Forex Patterns and Probabilities

Founded in 1807, John Wiley & Sons is the oldest independent publishing company in the United States. With offices in North America, Europe, Australia and Asia, Wiley is globally committed to developing and marketing print and electronic products and services for our customers' professional and personal knowledge and understanding.

The Wiley Trading series features books by traders who have survived the market's ever-changing temperament and have prospered—some by reinventing systems, others by getting back to basics. Whether a novice trader, professional, or somewhere in between, these books will provide the advice and strategies needed to prosper today and well into the future.

For a list of available titles, please visit our web site at www.WileyFinance.com.

Forex Patterns and Probabilities

Trading Strategies for Trending and
Range-Bound Markets

ED PONSI

John Wiley & Sons, Inc.

Published by John Wiley & Sons, Inc., Hoboken, New Jersey.
Published simultaneously in Canada.

Wiley Bicentennial Logo: Richard J. Pacifico

For general information on our other products and services or for technical support, please
contact our Customer Care Department within the United States at (800) 762-2974, outside the
United States at (317) 572-3993 or fax (317) 572-4002.

Wiley also publishes its books in a variety of electronic formats. Some content that appears in
print may not be available in electronic formats. For more information about Wiley products,
visit our web site at www.wiley.com.

Library of Congress Cataloging-in-Publication Data:

Ponsi, Ed, 1961–
  Forex patterns & probabilities : trading strategies for trending &
range-bound markets / Ed Ponsi.
      p.   cm. – (Wiley trading series)
  Includes index.
  ISBN 978-0-470-09729-8 (cloth)
  1. Foreign exchange market.   I. Title.   II. Title: Forex patterns and
probabilities.
  HG3851.P65   2007
  332.4'5–dc22

                                                    2007001693

Printed in the United States of America

10 9 8 7 6 5 4 3

To Mom, who taught me that anything is possible.

To Dad, who taught me the value of hard work.

Contents

Preface

M
ost books on trading deal with general concepts and shy away from specifics. There are plenty of books about the origins and history of currency trading, but very little in the way of useful, practical trading information. *Forex Patterns and Probabilities* provides readers with a rare sense of clarity about the specific mechanics of currency trading—real world strategies that tell the student when to enter, when to exit, and how to manage trades.

This book provides traders with step-by-step methodologies that are based on real market tendencies. The strategies in this book are presented clearly in great detail, so that anyone who wishes to can learn how to trade like a professional. It is written for the new or experienced trader who needs specific, useful information to trade the Forex market.

Forex Patterns and Probabilities begins with a whirlwind tour of life on a Wall Street trading desk, as the reader is transported to the exhilarating world of professional trading. Then, the author explains the "playing field" of the forex market, using powerful metaphors that relate trading scenarios to situations in everyday life.

Now that the reader has been sufficiently prepared, Ed unleashes several specific trading strategies designed for trending markets. Trends create some of the most highly profitable trading situations, and the reader is given an arsenal of specific techniques to profit from them. Ed's detailed explanations, backed by over 160 chart images, will leave no doubt in the mind of the reader exactly what the author is doing, and why he is doing it. Ed shares every part of his thought process, leaving nothing to the imagination.

Next, the book delves into a variety of trading techniques, all based on unique market tendencies. The author introduces the reader to the Ultimate Indicator, and the Keys to Intraday Breakouts. He then explains the proper usage of Triangles and Filters, and demonstrates the correct way to trade consolidation patterns such as Flags and Pennants. The dozens of chart examples and explanations allow the reader to "look over the shoulder" of a professional trader, hard at work at his craft.

Next, Ed introduces the volatility-based "Squeeze Play," and two day-trading techniques called the "Round Trip" and the "Boomerang." Yet another strategy, the "Interest Rate Edge," shows the reader how to trade like a hedge fund, revealing the techniques and philosophies used by the "smart money" to make fortunes.

Armed with this impressive arsenal of strategies and techniques, the reader is now presented with the means to turn this knowledge into power—and profit. In "How to Achieve Spectacular Gains," Ed shows exactly how professional traders make big money consistently, year after year. He then demonstrates the practical use of game theory in forex trading—a subject of immense importance, and a key to trading success.

In "What You Don't Know Can Hurt You," Ed gives an insider's insight into the pitfalls of forex trading and how to avoid them. Then, in "A Tale of Two Traders," the reader learns how to emulate the behavioral patterns of successful professional traders and how to escape the mind-set of the amateur.

Forex Patterns and Probabilities is packed with useful information from a Wall Street pro, yet it is written in an informal, easy-to-digest style that nearly anyone can understand.

Acknowledgments

I 'd like to thank everyone who helped to make the creation of this book a reality. In particular, I'd like to thank:

Kevin Commins, first for suggesting the writing of this book, and then for granting me the freedom to create something truly special and unique.

Emilie Herman, whose hard work and encouragement accentuated my strengths and concealed my weaknesses.

Josep Giró, an artist who fulfilled one of my lifelong dreams by turning me into an animated cartoon character.

And most of all, to my students, who constantly push me to be the very best forex trading instructor that I can be. Thank you one and all!

About the Author

E d Ponsi is the president of FXEducator.com and is the former chief trading instructor for Forex Capital Markets (FXCM). An experienced professional trader and money manager, Ed has advised hedge funds, institutional traders, and individuals of all levels of skill and experience. He is a regular contributor to FXStreet.com, TradingMarkets.com, and *SFO Magazine*, and has made numerous appearances on television, radio, online, and in print.

Ed's claim to fame is that he pulls no punches. His dynamic and humorous style of teaching sets him apart from the suit-and-tie crowd, making him one of the most sought-after lecturers in the financial world today. His no-nonsense, irreverent demeanor has earned him the moniker "The Rock Star of Forex Trading."

Ed's popular DVD series, "FXEducator: Forex Trading with Ed Ponsi" is now available at www.fxeducator.com and from select distributors worldwide. For more information, email us at info@fxeducator.com.

PART I

The World's Most Dynamic Trading Market

Trading the forex market is one of the most exciting and potentially profitable endeavors that you can undertake. We trade the entire world, matching the world's economies against one another. This market is vast, much larger than any stock or futures market. There is nothing else like it on earth.

The stakes are high; fortunes can be won or lost quickly. In order to succeed in this realm, we must first learn to understand it. . . .

CHAPTER 1

Getting Started in Forex

C *all me Ishmael...*
Just kidding. I'm sure that when anyone is blessed with the task of writing a book, that person secretly (or not so secretly) wishes that it might attain the status of a classic, like Melville's whaling tale.

You may be an experienced trader, or perhaps you're just starting out. Either way, remember: Everyone begins at the same starting point. Every trader who ever made money in any market began as a novice. Nobody is born with a deep, innate understanding of trading.

Maybe you believe that superior intelligence is required to succeed at trading. While being bright is not a disadvantage, it is no guarantee of success. Often, very intelligent traders overanalyze trading situations.

Maybe you believe that a good formal education is required to succeed, but this is not the case. What you are about to learn is not taught in any school. Traders learn through study, through trial and error, and through intense analysis of markets, strategies, and techniques. Most of all, traders learn through experience.

Maybe you believe that you must read every trading book you can find. I've read dozens of books on trading, most of which are not worth your time. Most of the books that I've read contained a kernel of useful information, buried beneath an avalanche of filler. I decided that if I were ever asked to write a book about trading, it would be the antithesis of those books. Instead of performing a sort of "Dance of the Seven Veils," I'd present an abundance of useful information in a way that most people could understand and appreciate.

My feeling is that the material is useless unless it is explained well, and my goal of helping you to succeed is best served by relating the concepts you are about to study to everyday life. This is a big part of my teaching technique, and you'll see it demonstrated repeatedly on these pages.

Perhaps you are wondering, "Where should I begin?"

FROM STOCKS TO FOREX

Like most traders in the United States, my first experiences involved stock trading. My first trade, 100 shares in a NASDAQ biotech stock, yielded a small loss.

I was lucky to have started out during the mid-1990s, during one of the most outstanding bull markets in history. In that environment, as long as a trader went with the trend, it was not too difficult to make money. It was a very forgiving market that would bail out even poor traders. The trick was to understand the difference between being good and merely being lucky. Many traders who I believed were talented began to falter when trading conditions became less than ideal. I realized that, like them, I had been a lucky trader, and that luck was transitory. I didn't want to be lucky; I wanted to become a good trader, one who could make money in any market environment. I wanted to work on Wall Street.

GETTING TO WALL STREET

After sending out dozens of resumes, I was interviewed and hired by a Wall Street firm as a trader. The fact that I didn't live in New York at the time was a minor detail, and soon I was getting up at around 4:00 A.M. to begin the trek to work.

I would exit my train beneath the World Trade Center, meet up with some coworkers for coffee, and grab copies of the *Wall Street Journal* and the *Investors Business Daily*. Once in the office, we would review dozens of charts, discuss recent market tendencies, study economic indicators—in short, we would do everything possible to prepare for the all-out war that would begin every day at 9:30 A.M.

Spending time in the Wall Street environment is an invaluable and irreplaceable experience. There were so many intelligent, driven people, with so much creative energy that you could feel it in the air like static electricity. We lived and breathed trading 24 hours per day, and learned concepts that changed the way we thought about the markets and trading, as well as the world in general. Much of what I learned in this environment would translate well to other trading markets, such as forex, and would become the basis for much of the material in this book.

Eventually, I was lured away by another firm and began working on another trading desk in Manhattan. I moved to New York City, shortening my daily commute from two hours each way to two blocks.

The new trading room was vast, with hundreds of desks and terminals. Having so many traders together, without walls or barriers to separate them, would facilitate the exchange of knowledge and information.

I sought out the best traders and questioned them relentlessly, absorbing and applying the information as quickly as possible. I was introduced to concepts that went far beyond anything I had seen earlier, and the pieces of the puzzle began to fall into place. I began to achieve a level of consistency that had been missing from my earlier trading, which had been profitable but erratic.

WELCOME TO THE JUNGLE

I also learned the disadvantages of trading in this environment, as there were too many people in the room expressing too many ideas and opinions. Essentially, it was a huge room full of ambitious and highly competitive alpha males. Some of the traders had egos that were out of control, and couldn't help but loudly express every mundane thought that rattled around their skulls. Others would merely express anger and frustration; the distinctive sound of a computer keyboard being smashed, along with the odd tinkling sound of letter keys flying through the air, is etched into my memory.

Jealousy reared its ugly head, as losing traders sought to distract and disrupt the winners. One trader took particular glee in trying to break my concentration, because he felt that my results were making him "look bad." If he had put as much effort into improving his own trading as he did into disrupting mine, he might have succeeded. He later left the firm to take a sales position.

Eventually, the market reached a point where the easy money had already been made. One by one, the marginal traders began to disappear. The market environment was changing, and traders would have to adapt to the changes or face failure.

FOOTBALL AND FOREX

One of the many benefits of living and working in New York City is exposure to people and cultures from around the world. One of the "new" concepts (at least it was new to me) to which I was exposed at this time was the currency market.

It was shocking to learn that foreign exchange trading, or forex, was tremendously popular in the rest of the world, and had been for many years. For most of the world, the forex market, not the stock market, is the market to trade. You could compare forex to football, which is the world's most popular sport—except in the United States, where it is considerably less popular and is referred to as "soccer." Here was a trading market that enjoyed wide popularity overseas, yet at the time it was "off the radar" in the United States.

A trader friend told me that he had decided to quit stock trading and instead switch to currencies, and that my style of trading would be perfectly suited to this new endeavor. I laughed, not knowing that soon I would make a similar move. Why on earth would I ever want to give up trading stocks?

STOCK MARKET HEADACHES

In life, there are certain unpleasantries with which we must learn to deal. We have to go to school, pay our bills, watch our weight, and so on. We accept these unpleasantries with thoughts such as "deal with it" or "that's life." After a while, we no longer think of these things as a burden; instead, they become the norm.

For equity traders, there are many unpleasant situations that are considered to be normal, just "part of the game." Stock traders don't think twice about these situations, because they are an ingrained part of their daily lives.

Partial Fills

For example, the "partial fill" is a normal occurrence in stock trading. A partial fill occurs when a trader places an order for a certain number of shares, let's say for 2,000 shares of stock, and instead receives only a portion of the order, for example, 300 shares. This happens all the time; the most logical explanation is that perhaps there were only 300 shares available at that particular price.

In trading terminology, we say that the market is too "thin" to absorb the entire order, meaning that there are not enough shares available at that price. This can be really frustrating, especially if the trader wants to enter large orders, but it is something that equity traders accept as normal, just another hurdle to overcome on the road to success.

The forex market, however, is highly liquid or "thick." Partial fills are extremely rare for all but the biggest traders.

Slippage

"Slippage" is another problem that stock and futures traders must deal with every day. Slippage is defined as "the difference between estimated transaction costs and the amount actually paid."

For example, suppose you purchased 1,000 shares of stock XYZ at a price of $50 per share. In order to protect yourself in the event that the price moves against you, you place a protective "stop" order (an order to sell) at $49. So your worst-case scenario is that you'll lose $1 per share, which in this case equals $1,000, right?

Wrong. If the price falls below $49 without touching the *exact price* of $49 (remember, stock markets are "thin" compared to forex), one of two things will happen. Either your order will not be executed at all, or it will be executed at a price *in the vicinity* of $49. Amazingly, the executed price is almost always less favorable than the price you desired! Slippage cuts into a trader's profits and is a major headache for stock and futures traders.

Slippage is rare in the currency market. Many forex market makers have a "no slippage" policy, giving currency traders a greater degree of price certainty.

The Specialist

Another hurdle to successful professional stock trading is the specialist. The specialist is a single individual who literally controls all of the trading activity of a listed stock. Early in my Wall Street career, I had an unforgettable trading experience that featured the specialist of a once high-flying stock that has since crashed in disgrace and scandal.

One day while trading shares listed on the New York Stock Exchange, I was long (meaning that I purchased shares in anticipation that the price would rise) 4,000 shares of stock, and the price began to fall toward my protective stop. Subsequently, the price reached my stop, and I took a small loss on my 4,000 shares. *Or so I thought. . . .*

Imagine my surprise when I looked at the computer screen to see that the stock was continuing its rapid descent, and I was still the unhappy owner of 3,900 shares. This was the day I learned that the specialist has the discretion to give a partial fill on a stop order.

Apparently, the specialist decided that the price was likely to continue falling (bad news about the company had just hit the newswire, obviously not for the last time), so he or she only filled my order by the minimum amount required (just 100 shares), leaving yours truly in a rather painful position.

There are no specialists in the forex market.

The Spread

In the stock market, the specialist also controls the spread (the difference between the buy and sell prices), and can widen or narrow the spread at his or her discretion. Since the specialist is trading against you, he can make your life miserable by widening the spread just as you are trying to exit a profitable trade. Gee, thanks, Mr. Specialist!

> In the forex market, the spread is often "fixed," allowing the trader a greater degree of certainty.

The "Uptick Rule"

Yet another frustrating roadblock to the success of equity traders is the "uptick rule." Stock traders can "go long" (place a trade that will become profitable if the stock rises) whenever they wish, but in order to "sell short" (place a trade that will become profitable if the stock falls), equity traders must go through a series of machinations that can prove both maddening and costly.

This rule requires that every short sale transaction be entered at a price that is at least equal to, or higher than, the price of the previous trade. The uptick rule prevents short sellers from adding to the downward momentum when the price of a stock is already experiencing a sharp decline. The problem this presents for the trader is that an opportunity to sell a stock short is often missed, because the stock was ticking down at the time, making it ineligible for a short sale.

In order to circumvent this rule, professional equity traders use various hybrid instruments known as *bullets, conversions,* or *married puts.* These instruments accomplish their intended task, but they are not always available, and they are not free. There is a cost involved—one of many that eats into the profits of equity traders.

There is no uptick rule in the forex market. You can buy or sell at will. There is no need to purchase bullets, conversions, or married puts.

WELCOME TO FOREX

While these impediments make stock trading more difficult than many of us would like, some good traders can and do overcome these hurdles. Yet I often hear stock traders complaining about how the specialist ruined their trade (in language that would scorch your ears), or how they've been "slipped" out of their profits, or that they placed a perfect entry, only to be foiled by a partial fill, or that they missed an opportunity to sell short because of the uptick rule.

What if these hurdles didn't exist? What if they were removed from the playing field, so that traders could relax and stop worrying, and instead get on with the business at hand? What if traders could just *trade? What would that be like?*

I was about to find out. One day after the closing bell, I had a few drinks with a trader friend who had quit the stock market to focus solely on the forex market. The conversation went something like this:

"It's called forex, short for foreign exchange. I just grab on to the trend and ride it for all it's worth."

"Haven't I seen that on TV? Something about green and red arrows?"

"Don't be a rube. When was the last time you saw someone on a trading floor looking at green and red arrows?"

"Okay, I get it. So what's so special about forex?"

"Ed, you've got to try this market! It's huge, it's liquid, and it's open for business 24 hours per day. You've never seen anything like it!"

"That's what I'm afraid of. I'm pretty happy right now trading stocks, so why would I want to switch to forex?"

"Because it's liquid! I can always get in, I can always get out, and I never get a partial fill."

"You never get a partial fill? Yeah, right."

"It hasn't happened yet. And I haven't been slipped yet either. My fills are always at the exact price where I place the order."

"You're lying! Where are you trading, in Disneyland?"

"You have no concept of how liquid this market is. It hardly ever gaps!"

"Okay, but how does it trade? Is it random, or does it trend?"

"That's the best part! The trends go on and on!"

"Kind of like you?"

"Very funny. If you don't believe me, open up a practice account and see for yourself."

"What are you talking about?"

"They have these practice accounts. You can trade real time, on their price feed, without any risk. It's a great way to get a feel for this market. It's free!"

"So I go to their office and trade their practice account while they try to sell me stuff, right? Sounds like a nightmare."

"No, genius, you trade the practice account from your home. You download it to your computer."

"Hmmm. No more tantrums. No more chair throwing. No more letter keys flying past my head while I try to decide if I should raise my stop. Maybe I'll give this market a shot."

A NEW BEGINNING

And so the journey began. As much as I used to enjoy trading stocks, I don't miss the headaches. It took a while to get used to the "feel" of the forex market, as it trades very differently from the way stocks trade. At first, I tried to trade forex the same exact way that I traded stocks, and for a few months I lost money. Once I adjusted to the different speed of the forex market, things eventually fell into place. You see, individual stocks move like jackrabbits—one moment they are standing still and the next moment they are zigzagging and flying around.

The forex market is huge compared to the stock market, so it takes a while longer for it to get moving. Once a currency pair does begin to move, it can continue moving in one direction for an incredibly long time.

The good news was that much of what I already knew about stock trading was transferable to the forex market. A chart was still a chart, and a trend was still a trend. The important concepts of risk management that I had learned from working on the equity desks in New York were still applicable.

At first, trading the forex market felt like visiting a foreign country. I was worried that it would feel as if I were visiting a distant planet. The difference in the market's reactions to economic news was startling. I was coming from an environment where traders had mere split seconds to react to news events. When trading stocks during a news release, if you don't get in right away, you are not likely to get in at all.

In the forex market, at first it almost seemed as if I had *too much* time to react to news and events. I actually had time to think about what was happening and to analyze the data. Better still, the forex market's reactions to news events usually made sense. As a certifiable "news junkie," it seemed that I had found the perfect trading vehicle.

It was almost too good to be true. It was a strange new market, yet something about it seemed so familiar. . . .

CHAPTER 2

All About Forex

I f you've ever traveled outside of your home country, there's a good chance that you've already performed a currency transaction. In most cases, travelers must exchange their "home" currency for the currency of the country they are visiting. Please note that there are two currencies involved in this transaction, but only one exchange rate.

For example, when a traveler from the United States crosses the border into Canada, he or she now must exchange U.S. dollars for Canadian dollars. This traveler is essentially selling the U.S. dollar and buying the Canadian dollar.

THE CANADIAN DOLLAR AND THE U.S. DOLLAR

In 2002, our traveler would have received about C$1.60 in Canadian currency for every U.S. dollar. We could say that the exchange rate at that time for the U.S. dollar/Canadian dollar was about 1.60 Canadian dollars per U.S. dollar. If we wanted to be precise, we could add several decimal spaces, and express the exchange rate as 1.6000.

In the years that followed, the exchange rate changed dramatically, and by 2006 it had fallen to 1.10. This meant that a traveler from the United States to Canada in 2006 would only receive about C$1.10 in Canadian currency for every U.S. dollar exchanged.

If we wanted to measure very small changes in this exchange rate, it could be expressed as 1.1000. We can safely say that the U.S. dollar depreciated significantly against the Canadian dollar during the early part of the twenty-first century (see Figure 2.1).

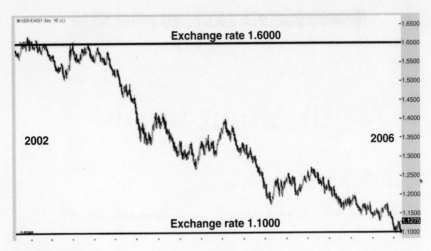

FIGURE 2.1 U.S. dollar/Canadian dollar exchange rate tumbles from 2002 through 2006.

Source: FXtrek IntelliChart™. Copyright © 2001–2006 FXtrek.com, Inc.

How does this affect our traveler? As the U.S. dollar/Canadian dollar exchange rate fell, U.S. dollars bought fewer Canadian goods and services.

A U.S. citizen landing in Toronto used to enjoy receiving a thick wad of cash from the airport's currency exchange kiosk. Visitors from the United States would spend freely, because goods and services seemed inexpensive compared to the prices at home.

As the Canadian dollar gained strength against the U.S. dollar, all of this changed. Eventually, the Canadian dollar approached parity to the U.S. dollar.

While this had a negative impact on visitors from the United States, Canadian travelers were pleased to find that U.S. goods and services were now relatively cheap. As the U.S. dollar weakened, the comparative buying power of the Canadian dollar grew.

U.S. citizens were now less likely to visit Canada. If they did, they were likely to spend less than they would have in the past, when the exchange rate was more favorable. Canadian travelers, however, were more likely to visit the United States, since the Canadian currency bought more U.S. goods and services than it had previously.

THE EURO AND THE U.S. DOLLAR

The rise of the euro created a similar situation. The euro made dramatic gains against the U.S. dollar in 2002, 2003, and 2004, and during that time

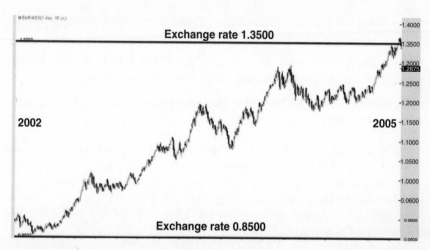

FIGURE 2.2 Euro/U.S. dollar exchange rate climbs from 2002 through 2005.

Source: FXtrek IntelliChart™. Copyright © 2001–2006 FXtrek.com, Inc.

the value of the euro rose from about US$0.85 cents to above US$1.35 (see Figure 2.2). Due to this shift in exchange rates, U.S. citizens found that vacationing in Europe became much more expensive, while persons visiting the United States from Europe found that their buying power had increased dramatically.

This resulted in a huge influx of shoppers from Europe visiting the United States, especially around the Christmas holiday season. One European trader explained to me that it was less expensive for him to fly to New York City, stay in a hotel, shop, and return home than it would be to simply stay at home and shop.

While there can be no doubt that fortunes were made and lost on the huge movements described above, we will see how even a tiny move in exchange rates can result in substantial gains or losses. This is how forex traders make money.

TRADING TERMINOLOGY

Traders have their own language. They use words that might confuse a "newbie" or a nontrader. Trading lingo is almost a type of secret handshake that lets other traders know that you're a member of the club.

There is a method to the madness of trading terminology. Many of these terms allow a trader to express a concise thought in one or two quick syllables. In any discussion involving trading, you'll often hear the terms *long*, *short*, and *flat*. In fact, every trader is always long, short, or flat. What do these terms mean?

Going long. When a trader says he is "going long," he is placing a trade that will become profitable if the exchange rate rises.

Selling short. When a trader says he is "going short" or "selling short," he is placing a trade that will become profitable if the exchange rate falls.

Flat. When a trader says he is "flat," he is neither long nor short. This trader has no open positions in the market.

Why do traders use these terms? Why not just use the word *buy* instead of *long*, and use the word *sell* instead of *short*?

The answer is simple when you consider that traders can make money whether the exchange rate moves up or down. For example, suppose you walk into my office and ask me what sort of trade I will be making today. I tell you that I'm going to sell today.

Isn't it true that the word *sell* could have two different meanings? Perhaps I'm going to sell a currency pair that I bought last week, in order to take a profit. Or it could mean that I'm opening a short trade; in other words, I'm selling a currency pair today in order to profit from an expected drop in the exchange rate.

However, if you ask that same question of me and I answer, "I'm going short," there can be no confusion as to my meaning. If I'm selling short, I am definitely going to make money if the exchange rate falls, and I'm definitely going to lose money if the exchange rate rises. There can be no doubt about it.

Suppose you ask me what I am planning to do today, and I tell you that I plan to buy. Again, this word has two potential meanings. Perhaps I'm going to buy because I think the exchange rate is going to rise. Or it could be that I sold short last week, and the exchange rate has fallen. In order to take a profit and "close" the trade, I have to buy back the currency pair that I sold short last week. This is called "covering a short."

If I do cover my short position, and I have no other open trades, I will be "flat." I will have no open positions in the market.

If I were to tell you, "I'm going long today," this can have only one meaning. It means that if the exchange rate rises, I'll make a profit, and if it falls, I'll lose money. The use of these terms removes ambiguity because they describe trading activity in precise terms.

What Is a Pip?

A pip is the smallest increment of price in the forex market. It is an acronym for the phrase "percentage in point." You might recall that in an earlier example, the exchange rate for the U.S. dollar/Canadian dollar currency pair was 1.10, and we expanded that to 1.1000 for the sake of precise measurement.

The reason why this is a more precise representation is that it allows us to show the smallest possible increment of change in the exchange rate. For example, suppose the exchange rate rises from 1.1000 to 1.1001. We could say that the exchange rate rose by one pip—the smallest increment of change possible.

The Major Currencies

Here is a list of some of the most actively traded currencies and their currency codes. Please note that this is a partial list, as there are many currencies traded in the world today:

EUR = euro
GBP = Great Britain pound
USD = U.S. dollar
JPY = Japanese yen
CHF = Swiss franc
CAD = Canadian dollar
AUD = Australian dollar
NZD = New Zealand dollar

Nicknames

Many of these currencies possess colorful nicknames. Traders love to use slang, so you need to know these nicknames in order to understand what they are saying. Here are some examples:

U.S. dollar	"greenback" or "buck"
British pound	"cable" or "sterling"
Euro	"single currency"
Swiss franc	"Swissy"
Canadian dollar	"loonie"
Australian dollar	"Aussie"
New Zealand dollar	"kiwi"

The origins of these nicknames are an interesting topic of discussion. For example, the euro is called the single currency because it is one currency that is used by many countries. A "kiwi" is a flightless, nocturnal bird, and is also a national symbol of New Zealand.

Long ago, the Great Britain pound was considered the world's dominant currency, and British pounds were frequently wired back and forth between North America and Europe via the transatlantic cable. Many years later, the nickname "cable" persists. The pound was originally equal in value to one pound in weight of sterling silver, hence the term "pound sterling" or simply "sterling."

"Loonie" is the unofficial but commonly used name for Canada's gold-colored, bronze-plated, one-dollar coin. The nickname is derived from the picture of a loon, a distinctive bird, on one side of the coin.

Central Banks

Every country (or in the case of Europe, a group of countries) has a corresponding interest rate, and that rate is determined by a central bank. Forex traders monitor interest rates carefully, because they have a dramatic impact on currency exchange rates.

> European Union: European Central Bank (ECB)
> United Kingdom: Bank of England (BoE)
> United States: Federal Reserve (Fed)
> Japan: Bank of Japan (BoJ)
> Switzerland: Swiss National Bank (SNB)
> Canada: Bank of Canada (BoC)
> Australia: Reserve Bank of Australia (RBA)
> New Zealand: Reserve Bank of New Zealand (RBNZ)

These central banks raise interest rates to fight inflation, and lower interest rates to stimulate growth. Their actions create movements in exchange rates that are instrumental in many forex trading strategies.

Popular Currency Pairs

Here are some of the most popular currency pairs:

EUR/USD	**Euro–U.S. dollar**
USD/JPY	U.S. dollar–Japanese yen
GBP/USD	Great Britain pound–U.S. dollar
USD/CHF	U.S. dollar–Swiss franc
AUD/USD	Australian dollar–U.S. dollar
USD/CAD	U.S. dollar–Canadian dollar
NZD/USD	New Zealand dollar–U.S. dollar
EUR/JPY	Euro–Japanese yen
EUR/GBP	Euro–Great Britain pound
GBP/CHF	Great Britain pound–Swiss Franc
EUR/AUD	Euro–Australian dollar

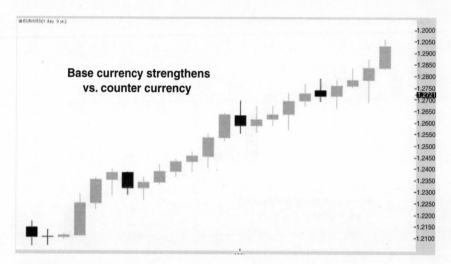

FIGURE 2.3 Base currency strengthens in relation to the counter currency.

Source: FXtrek IntelliChart™. Copyright © 2001–2006 FXtrek.com, Inc.

The first member of every currency pair is called the "base" currency, and the second member of each pair is known as the "quote" or "counter" currency. For example, in the case of the euro/U.S. dollar currency pair (EUR/USD), the euro is the base member of the pair, and the U.S. dollar is the counter member of the pair.

In order to prevent confusion, the currencies in the EUR/USD pair should always be presented in their correct order. You won't see this pair represented as USD/EUR, unless you are trading currency futures.

Who decides which currency is the base currency, and which is the counter or quote currency? That task falls to the International Organization for Standardization, or ISO. The ISO determines the currency codes and the order of the currencies within each pair.

Whenever a currency pair is rising on a chart, this means that the base currency is strengthening versus the counter currency. This is true for every currency pair (see Figure 2.3).

The opposite is also true—if the base currency is growing weaker versus the counter currency, the chart will show the exchange rate of that currency pair falling (see Figure 2.4).

Lots

In the stock market, traders buy and sell shares. In the futures market, traders buy and sell contracts. In the forex market, traders buy and sell

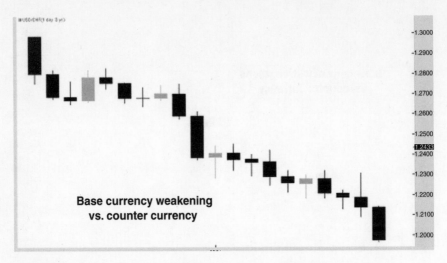

FIGURE 2.4   Base currency weakens in relation to the counter currency.

Source: FXtrek IntelliChart™. Copyright © 2001–2006 FXtrek.com, Inc.

"lots." The smallest position that a trader can take in the forex market is "one lot."

Each lot consists of 100,000 units of currency. So if you are long one lot of the EUR/USD currency pair, in reality you are long 100,000 units of the base currency and short 100,000 units of the counter or quote currency. Therefore, a trader who is long one lot of the EUR/USD currency pair is actually long 100,000 euros, and simultaneously short an equivalent amount of U.S. dollars.

Entry

The entry or entry point is the point at which a long or short position is opened. This is where the trade begins.

Stop or Protective Stop

A stop order is an order that is placed to exit a trade if the exchange rate makes an unfavorable move. This is done to keep losses minimal and under control.

Target

A target is placed to exit a position if the exchange rate makes a favorable move. It is also referred to as a "take-profit" order.

Spot or Cash Market

The spot price is the value of an object or item right now, or "on the spot." This differs from a futures contract, which places a value on an object or item in the future.

For example, suppose you want to buy a bottle of water. You are thirsty, so you want the water right now. The person behind the counter charges you $1 for a bottle of water. Therefore, $1 is the "spot" price of water at that store—the price you will pay right now, or "on the spot."

On the other hand, suppose you want to lock in a price for water that you'll need in the *future*. You negotiate with the storeowner, taking inflation, supply and demand, and future uncertainty into consideration. You agree on a price of $1.05. You have now entered into a *futures* contract for water.

When you see a reference to the "spot" or "cash" forex market, this is done to differentiate between the current (spot) market and the future (futures) market.

Liquid

A liquid or "thick" market is a market in which selling and buying can be accomplished with ease. This is because there are more buyers and sellers in a liquid market like forex. A market with few buyers and sellers is referred to as "illiquid."

Leverage

Leverage is the ability to control a large amount of capital with a comparatively small amount of capital.

For example, one lot of a currency pair has a value of 100,000 units of currency—100,000 euros or 100,000 U.S. dollars, and so on. Do we actually need to possess 100,000 euros or 100,000 U.S. dollars in order to trade one lot of the EUR/USD currency pair?

No, we can control one lot with as little as 1/200th of that amount. We could say that a person who controls one lot in this fashion is using 200-to-1 leverage. The amount of leverage used by traders varies based on their individual needs and their "comfort zone."

Support

Support is a point on the chart where the exchange rate has shown a tendency to stop falling. Support is not an exact price point, but an area. Think of support as the floor beneath you (see Figure 2.5).

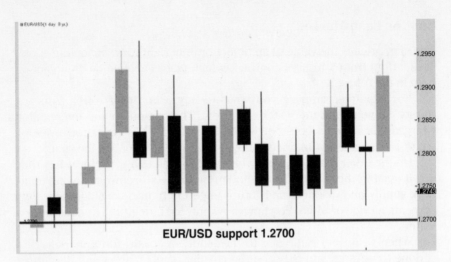

FIGURE 2.5 The euro/U.S. dollar currency pair finds support repeatedly near 1.2700.

Source: FXtrek IntelliChart™. Copyright © 2001–2006 FXtrek.com, Inc.

Resistance

Resistance is a point on the chart where the exchange rate has shown a tendency to stop rising. Like support, resistance is an area, not an exact price level. Think of resistance as the ceiling above you (see Figure 2.6).

Breakout

A breakout occurs when the exchange rate breaks beneath support or above resistance (see Figure 2.7).

Trend

A trend occurs when the exchange rate moves consistently in one direction, either higher or lower (see Figure 2.8).

Range

A range occurs when the exchange rate has no clear direction and is contained within visible support and resistance levels (see Figure 2.9).

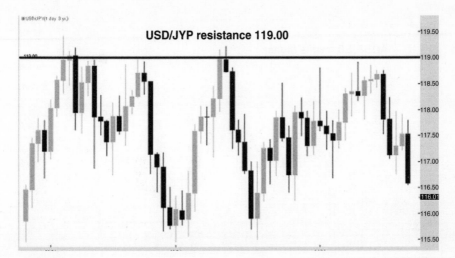

FIGURE 2.6 The U.S. dollar/Japanese yen pair finds resistance repeatedly near 119.00.

Source: FXtrek IntelliChart™. Copyright © 2001–2006 FXtrek.com, Inc.

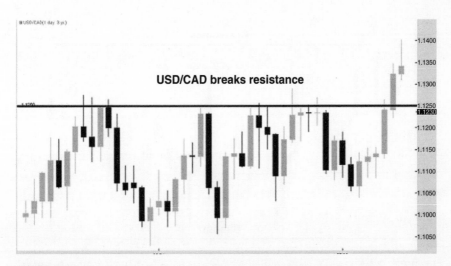

FIGURE 2.7 Breakout in the U.S. dollar/Canadian dollar currency pair.

Source: FXtrek IntelliChart™. Copyright © 2001–2006 FXtrek.com, Inc.

FIGURE 2.8 A trend forms in the Australian dollar/U.S. dollar currency pair.

Source: FXtrek IntelliChart™. Copyright © 2001–2006 FXtrek.com, Inc.

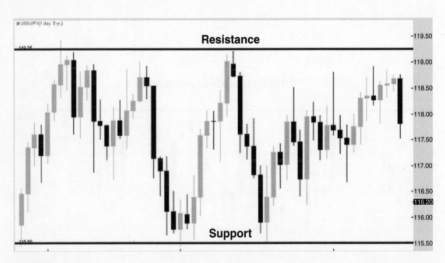

FIGURE 2.9 The U.S. dollar/Japanese yen pair bounces between support and resistance.

Source: FXtrek IntelliChart™. Copyright © 2001–2006 FXtrek.com, Inc.

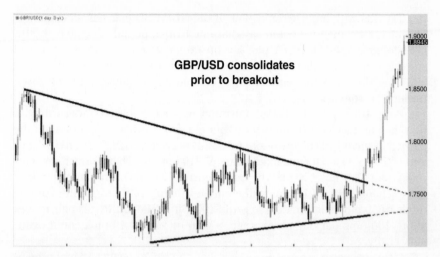

FIGURE 2.10 The Great Britain pound/U.S. dollar pair consolidates prior to a breakout.

Source: FXtrek IntelliChart™. Copyright © 2001–2006 FXtrek.com, Inc.

Consolidation

A consolidation occurs when the exchange rate is trapped in an ever-narrowing area. Consolidations often lead to breakouts (see Figure 2.10).

Volatility

Volatility is a measure of the amount by which a currency pair is expected to fluctuate over a given period. A volatile currency pair tends to make rapid, forceful moves, while a pair that lacks volatility tends to trade in a more predictable fashion.

AN EASY WAY TO UNDERSTAND THE EXCHANGE RATE

It's easier to understand exchange rates if you think of the base currency as the number "one." For example, suppose that the exchange rate for EUR/USD is 1.2904. The base currency is the euro, because that is the first member of the pair. Think of the euro as the number "one," as in "one euro equals 1.2904 U.S. dollars." This means that one euro would be worth about $1.29 in U.S. dollars.

Try this with any currency pair. If the GBP/USD pair has an exchange rate of 1.9012, then we could say that one British pound is equal to 1.9012 U.S. dollars. If the USD/JPY pair has an exchange rate of 115.00, we could say that one U.S. dollar is equal in value to exactly 115 Japanese yen.

How do these movements in exchange rates translate to the forex trader's bottom line?

When trading the EUR/USD currency pair, a U.S.-based trader will note that the pair has a fixed value of $10 per pip. In fact, this is true for all of the pairs that have USD as the quote (second) currency. GBP/USD, AUD/USD, and NZD/USD also have a fixed value of $10 per pip. Therefore, in any currency pair that has USD as the quote currency, a favorable movement in the exchange rate of 10 pips will create a gain of $100, and an unfavorable move of 10 pips will create a loss of $100. Since the EUR/USD pair moves about 100 pips per day on average, a gain or loss of 10 pips could occur very easily.

If this scenario creates more risk than the trader wishes to incur, he or she could open a "mini" account. In a mini account, the EUR/USD currency pair has a constant pip value of $1. In this case, a favorable movement in the exchange rate of 10 pips would create a gain of $10, and an unfavorable move of 10 pips would create a loss of $10.

By this point, you've learned quite a bit about forex, but you probably have a few questions. . . .

CHAPTER 3

Questions and Answers

F orex differs from any other market, and traders must first understand it in order to trade successfully. Along the way, some questions will inevitably occur. In this chapter, I answer some of the most common questions about forex.

WHY DOES THE BIG MONEY TRADE FOREX?

The forex market (which goes by many names, including FX, foreign exchange, the global market, and the currency market) may seem like the new kid on the block, but it has been the market of choice for global hedge funds and institutional investors for years. The "big money" has always traded forex, because the huge size of the market allows these traders to enter and exit large trades without creating price distortions and disrupting exchange rates. Yet this market seems brand new to many individual traders, because the barriers to entry that used to keep the little guy out of the forex market have only recently fallen away.

In the past few years, the popularity of forex trading has taken off—and for good reason. The forex market's daily volume, estimated at about U.S.$1.9 trillion and growing, is unmatched by any trading market in the world.

Forex traders also have the ability to use tremendous leverage, which can be greater than 200-to-1. Leverage allows a trader to "magnify" his or her trading positions, and also serves to magnify gains and losses.

Compare this to a typical stock trading account, which normally has leverage of about 2-to-1. Because of this superior leverage, the barriers to entry for forex traders are very low. Traders can open accounts with as little as a few hundred dollars.

WHY IS FOREX SUDDENLY SO POPULAR?

Traditionally, access to this market had been restricted to major corporations, hedge funds, and other institutional investors. Most of the world's major banks are heavily involved in the foreign exchange market and have been for years. Until recently, the individual trader had no way to access this market, because there was no way to compete with the "big boys" on a level playing field.

In the 1990s, the forex market was finally able to open its doors to retail clientele. Online forex market makers opened the gates (and made fortunes), by breaking huge trading positions into "bite-sized chunks" that individuals could buy and sell.

This means that individuals can now trade alongside the biggest banks in the world and even use the same techniques and strategies that professional traders use. Suddenly, the trading landscape has changed, and traders have a "new" alternative to stock and futures markets.

HOW DO TRADERS MAKE MONEY IN THE FOREX MARKET?

Currency traders simply attempt to profit from changes in the exchange rate. Because of the tremendous leverage available to forex traders, a very small change in the exchange rate can result in a large profit or loss.

Fortunes can be made or lost quickly in this market; even a move in the exchange rate that is equivalent to a few hundredths of a penny can be magnified into a substantial gain or loss.

Most traders consider themselves members of one of two major categories, technical traders and fundamental traders. *Technical traders* focus on technical analysis, which is the study of charts (historic price action) and indicators, to trade forex. They believe that all of the pertinent information needed to place a trade is contained within the chart.

Fundamental traders use fundamental analysis, which we can loosely describe as the study of economics (especially interest rates) to trade the forex market. They believe that currencies will eventually become stronger or weaker in response to their underlying economic strength or weakness, and due to changes in interest rates and monetary policy.

Most individuals are interested in the technical aspects of currency trading and have a tendency to feel intimidated when it comes to fundamental analysis. This is probably because charts are a visual device for pattern recognition, and can be interpreted quickly with experience.

Meanwhile, economics is a subject that is usually presented in a manner that can best be described as wordy and boring. Hey, there's a reason why economics is called "the dismal science"!

Don't be intimidated by economics and fundamentals. Generally, the fault is not with the subject, but with the manner of presentation.

While this book primarily deals with the technical strategies and techniques of forex trading, I want to encourage you to think of the technical and fundamental aspects of forex as intertwined. In other words, what you see on the chart (technical) didn't just appear by chance—it is there for a reason (fundamental).

Unfortunately, most traders tend to look at technical and fundamental analysis as an either/or proposition, but for now I just want to encourage you to consider that they are not mutually exclusive. We'll cover this concept in greater detail as we progress through some trading techniques.

WHY DO CURRENCIES TRADE IN PAIRS?

This is a concept that many students find confusing at first, but it's actually very simple. Whenever you enter a currency trade, there are two currencies involved. Think about the traveler from our earlier discussion, who exchanged his homeland's currency for the currency of the land he was visiting. You'll recall that there were two currencies involved in the transaction, but only one exchange rate.

Every foreign exchange transaction, or forex trade, involves two currencies and one exchange rate. The best way to illustrate the reason for this is to attempt to initiate a currency transaction that involves just one currency. For example, if you live in the United States, walk down to your local grocery store and ask the person behind the counter, "How many U.S. dollars will you give me in exchange for 20 U.S. dollars?"

After the clerk gives you a sideways look, he'll assume that you want change for a twenty, and $20 is exactly what you'll get—no more and no less. Nobody is going to offer you more than $20 for a $20 bill, so you cannot profit from this exchange.

Imagine the difficulty involved in trying to trade just one currency. Will any sane person offer more than one British pound in exchange for another

British pound? Remember, we are not speaking about collectible coins or interest-bearing loans, just a pure currency exchange.

Conversely, a clever trader might offer less than one British pound in exchange for one British pound, but only a fool would accept this proposition. This explains why we cannot trade just one currency at a time.

This is because the value of a currency *itself* does not change, but its value can change in relation to *another* currency. In other words, that dollar in your pocket will still be worth $1 tomorrow; however, its value constantly fluctuates *relative* to other currencies. This is why we must trade currencies in pairs.

HOW CAN I TRADE TWO CURRENCIES AT ONE TIME?

Many traders find it helpful to think of a currency pair as a single instrument, just like a stock. For example, if an equity trader believes that IBM stock will rise in value, that trader will "go long" IBM stock.

Similarly, if a forex trader believes that the euro will rise against the U.S. dollar, that trader can "go long" the euro/U.S. dollar currency pair. If the same trader believed that the euro might weaken against the U.S. dollar, he or she could "sell short" the euro/U.S. dollar currency pair.

You might hear a currency trader say, "I'm buying the dollar" or "I'm selling the euro." It may sound as if this individual is trading just one currency, but he or she is actually trading two currencies. If you are trading the U.S. dollar, the euro, or any currency, you are trading it against another currency.

HOW IS 24-HOUR-PER-DAY TRADING POSSIBLE?

One of the major advantages of the spot forex market is the fact that it is a seamless, 24-hour trading market. Instead of conforming to a rigid schedule, traders can decide for themselves when to trade, whether it is morning, afternoon, or night.

Even part-time traders who work full-time jobs can trade forex. No matter where you are located in the world, no matter what hours you keep, you can trade the forex market.

When we're dealing with a vast, liquid market like forex, it's important to understand which times of day are the most active. This is especially important when we place intraday trades—trades that are intended to have a short duration.

HOW IS THE TRADING DAY STRUCTURED?

Since the forex market is open 24 hours per day, we can't really say that the market opens or closes at a particular time of day. Unlike stock and futures markets, there is no "opening bell."

Since we'll be working with charts that require an opening price and a closing price, forex traders must designate a particular time of day as a benchmark.

For most traders, the forex trading day begins at 5:00 P.M. Eastern U.S. (New York) time, 10:00 P.M. London time. Because forex trades 24 hours per day, the trading day also ends at 5:00 P.M. New York time, 10:00 P.M. London time.

Why is this particular time used? Consider that when it is 5:00 P.M. on Sunday in New York, it is Monday morning in Australia and New Zealand. According to the International Date Line, Monday morning reaches this part of the world before any other active forex trading area. Hence, it marks the beginning of the trading day.

Overall, volume is low at this time of day because the three biggest forex trading centers—Great Britain, the United States, and Japan—are quiet at this time. However, the Australian dollar and the New Zealand dollar may see some action during these hours.

The Asian Session

A few hours later, at around 7:00 P.M. Eastern U.S. time, midnight London time, Japan awakens and the forex markets begin to stir. This is considered the beginning of the Asian session.

Japan is the third largest forex trading center, and comprises about 10 percent of all forex trading volume. Many of the world's major banks and hedge funds have offices in Tokyo. Activity in the Japanese yen pairs begins to surge at this time of day.

The European Session

As the Asian trading day winds down around 3:00 A.M. Eastern U.S. time, European markets open for business, and the London trading day begins soon afterward. This is considered to be the beginning of the European session.

Great Britain is by far the most important forex trading market on the planet, and London is considered the world's capital of forex trading. Roughly 30 percent of all foreign exchange volume comes from the trading desks of London.

The U.S. Session

At around 8:00 A.M. New York time, about halfway through the London trading session, U.S. forex traders come to life. This is considered to be the beginning of the U.S. trading session. New York is the second most important market in forex trading, and accounts for about 15 percent of the world's total foreign exchange volume.

Trading is especially active early in the U.S. session, as it overlaps the European session. Now the two giants of forex, London and New York, are both in play at the same time.

U.S. economic news releases occur in the early part of this session and can cause a tremendous amount of volatility. Exchange rates swing wildly as the market digests this new information.

Trading usually becomes aimless and choppy after midday in New York as the London session winds down, and liquidity and volatility begin to dissipate. By mid to late afternoon New York time, London traders have gone home for the day, and it is late at night in Japan. New York traders, while still active at this time of day, have already finished with the bulk of their trading.

Friday afternoons in the United States are generally the least active, because for much of the trading world, it is already Friday night or Saturday. The reduced liquidity often leads to "choppy" movements, because in an illiquid environment, orders that normally would not have the power to move exchange rates now can do exactly that.

Finally, as the U.S. markets close, a new trading day is just about to begin in the western Pacific. The Australian and New Zealand markets begin to stir, starting the process once again. The cycle continues all week, with most trading desks closed from Friday afternoon until Sunday afternoon, Eastern U.S. time.

GREENWICH MEAN TIME

How do forex traders keep track of all of these various times of day? Because forex traders are located everywhere in the world, they use Greenwich Mean Time (GMT) so that all traders can have a common point of reference.

TABLE 3.1 Active Forex Trading Times for Various Parts of the World

Forex Market	Becomes Active	Becomes Inactive
Australia/New Zealand	2100 GMT	500 GMT
Japan/Asia	2300 GMT	700 GMT
Europe/Great Britain	700 GMT	1600 GMT
United States/Canada	1200 GMT	2100 GMT

Depending on the time of the year, Greenwich Mean Time is either four hours or five hours ahead of U.S. Eastern time. This is because GMT does not recognize Daylight Saving Time.

It's easy to keep track of Greenwich Mean Time once you get used to it, and many forex trading platforms include a digital GMT clock for your convenience. Table 3.1 shows the forex trading day, according to Greenwich Mean Time.

CHAPTER 4

Technical Analysis and the Forex Market

Why have so many former equity and futures traders chosen to trade in the currency markets? Many have discovered that technical analysis works exceptionally well in the forex markets, and are reaping the benefits of trading in the global marketplace. Why does technical analysis work so well in the forex market? Technical analysis is simply the analysis of past price movements to help predict future price movements. In many cases, a trader using technical analysis is simply looking for the repetition of past occurrences.

This chapter explains how traders use this technique to optimal effectiveness in the currency markets.

THE THEORY BEHIND TECHNICAL ANALYSIS

Long-term movements in the currency market generally correlate with economic cycles. These economic cycles tend to repeat themselves, and so they can be predicted with a reasonable degree of accuracy. Repetition is the key, since the entire premise of technical analysis lies in using historical price movement to predict future price movement.

In the stock market, the fundamentals of a particular company can change radically in a short period of time. This makes past stock prices irrelevant in the prediction of future movement. There is no predictable economic cycle in the life of a company or in the life of an individual stock. As a result, technical analysis becomes a hit-or-miss proposition in the stock market.

In the forex market, we are trading the economies of entire countries. The fundamentals of these countries change very slowly, making the boom-bust nature of the economic cycle easier to predict.

STATISTICAL SURVEY

Which would you consider more accurate—a survey of five people or a survey of 5,000 people? If the survey is performed in a fair and even-handed manner, the larger sample of information will generally reveal the more accurate result.

The greater size and liquidity of the forex market gives technical analysts a larger sample of information from which to draw. There are many more trades, and much more money changing hands than in any stock market or futures market. The currency market contains more data points, making a statistical sampling like technical analysis more accurate.

Also, the vast liquidity found in the currency market makes it much less likely that insignificant players will disrupt the market and temporarily skew technical indicators, which is common in less liquid markets. One stock trader can easily influence the price of an illiquid stock, but it is much more difficult—and expensive—to exert influence over exchange rates.

For example, imagine a stock that trades an average daily volume of just 20,000 shares per day. If a trader places a market order to buy 10,000 shares of this stock, what do you think will happen? Because this order is equal to 50 percent of the stock's average daily volume, the price rockets higher, as the available offers are absorbed. In a very real sense, one trader has single-handedly moved the market for that stock.

While this scenario is common in the equity markets, it is unheard of in the currency markets. The sheer size of the forex market makes this type of reaction nearly impossible. In fact, there have been numerous occasions where governments and central banks have tried to exert their influence over currency exchange rates and failed.

FEAR OF THE UNKNOWN

It's natural to have a fear of the unknown, and this is normal human behavior. I remember when I first decided to get involved with forex trading, there were many concerns weighing on my mind. What would the chart look like? Would I have to abandon my current trading style and learn some esoteric new method of trading?

These are common concerns of traders who want to experience the advantages of forex, but are reluctant to leave their "comfort zone." As we take a look at charts of forex exchange rates, the first thing that will become apparent is that they are not very different from the charts of other trading vehicles, such as stocks or commodities.

TRADING PATTERNS AND TECHNICAL INDICATORS

For experienced equities and futures traders, the good news is that nearly everything you already know about technical analysis can be applied to the forex market. Forex charts contain familiar patterns like the head and shoulders, double tops and double bottoms, and symmetrical and asymmetrical triangles.

Forex traders use moving averages, Bollinger bands, moving average convergence/divergence (MACD)—all of the same indicators that equity and futures traders use. There are breakouts and pullbacks, retracements and consolidations, ranges and trends. For example, Figure 4.1 shows a pattern that is familiar to traders who use technical analysis—a double top formation in the euro/USD (euro/U.S. dollar) currency pair.

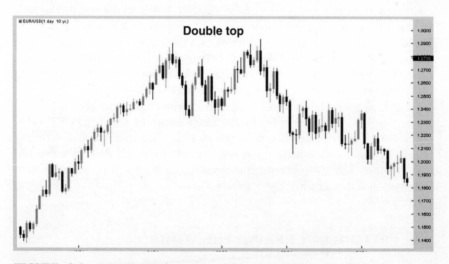

FIGURE 4.1 A double-top formation in the EUR/USD currency pair.

Source: FXtrek IntelliChart™. Copyright © 2001–2006 FXtrek.com, Inc.

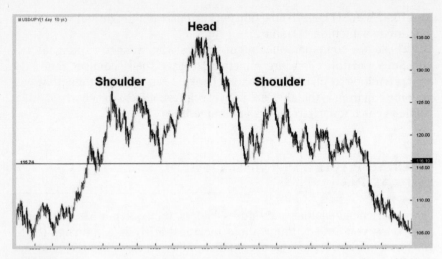

FIGURE 4.2 A massive head-and-shoulders formation in the USD/JPY currency pair.

Source: FXtrek IntelliChart™. Copyright © 2001–2006 FXtrek.com, Inc.

Experienced traders of stocks and commodities will see many familiar formations and patterns in the charts of currency pairs. For example, take a look at the massive head-and-shoulders pattern that formed over a three-year period in the USD/JPY (U.S. dollar/Japanese yen) currency pair (Figure 4.2).

Forex traders use support and resistance levels to determine the best location for entry and stop orders, just like equity and futures traders. In Figure 4.3, the USD/CAD (U.S. dollar/Canadian dollar) currency pair finds support repeatedly at the 1.2000 level. Traders who are familiar with candlestick charting patterns will note the series of hammers, dojis, spinning tops, and other reversal candles at the support level.

Strategies involving trend lines and channels are also popular in the forex markets. For example, in the daily chart of the USD/CHF (U.S. dollar/Swiss franc) currency pair, we can see two distinct and separate channels, one moving higher and one moving lower. Note that when the first channel fails, the uptrend dissolves into a double top, which is then followed by a downtrend (see Figure 4.4).

THE PSYCHOLOGY BEHIND THE MARKET

One of the great advantages of technical analysis is that it gives us insight into the mind-set of that market's participants. When we see a particular

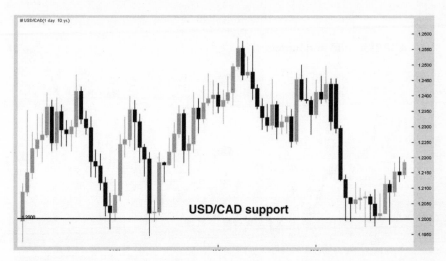

FIGURE 4.3 USD/CAD finds support repeatedly near the vicinity of 1.2000.

Source: FXtrek IntelliChart™. Copyright © 2001–2006 FXtrek.com, Inc.

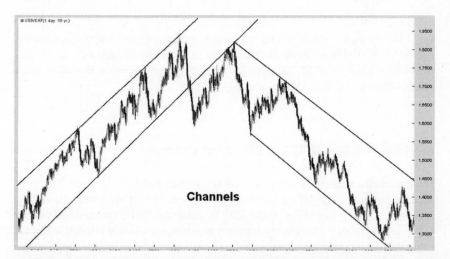

FIGURE 4.4 Two distinct channels form in the USD/CHF currency pair.

Source: FXtrek IntelliChart™. Copyright © 2001–2006 FXtrek.com, Inc.

formation on the chart, we know that this is a visual manifestation of the psychology behind the market. The reason for this is that, although the participants may change, human nature remains constant. The same human psychology that creates technical patterns in equities and futures charts is also at work in the forex market, so the same patterns appear.

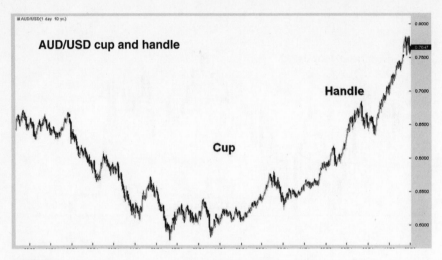

FIGURE 4.5 A massive cup-and-handle formation in the AUD/USD pair.

Source: FXtrek IntelliChart™. Copyright © 2001–2006 FXtrek.com, Inc.

For example, stock traders who favor the cup-and-handle formation will also find this pattern in the forex market. In Figure 4.5, we see a massive cup-and-handle pattern, followed by a breakout in the AUD/USD (Australian dollar/U.S. dollar) currency pair.

MOVING BEYOND TECHNICAL ANALYSIS

It's important to remember that underlying fundamentals create the technical picture we see when we look at a chart. When we trade forex, we are not trading companies, but entire economies. The fundamentals of an individual country's economy change much more slowly than the fundamentals of an individual company.

If the stock of an individual company is weak, there are a variety of actions that can be taken. For example, we can replace the CEO, restructure the company, add new members to the board of directors, and so on, and turn the company around quickly.

Turning around the fortunes of an entire country is a much more complicated and time-consuming process. For this reason, the repetition of the technical patterns we seek is much more likely to occur on the chart of a currency pair than on a stock chart. It's also the reason why trends tend to continue for months and even years in the forex market.

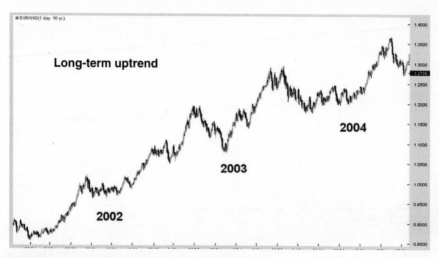

FIGURE 4.6 A long-term uptrend in the EUR/USD currency pair.

Source: FXtrek IntelliChart™. Copyright © 2001–2006 FXtrek.com, Inc.

TRENDS

Currency pairs have a tendency to form strong, persistent trends. The forex market is famous for these trends, and they are the main reason why trend-following traders are drawn to this market.

For example, the euro trended consistently higher against the U.S. dollar over a three-year period. This uptrend occurred during a period of U.S. economic weakness (see Figure 4.6).

PROPER ORDER

One way to determine if a pair is trending is through the use of moving averages, and what is referred to as the "proper order" of moving averages. Let's define the proper order for an uptrend as: the 10-period *simple moving average (SMA)* is located above the 20-period SMA, which is above the 50-period SMA, which is above the 200-period SMA:

$$10 > 20 > 50 > 200$$

The order would be reversed in the case of a downtrend:

$$200 > 50 > 20 > 10$$

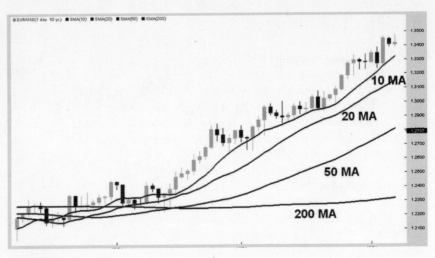

FIGURE 4.7 EUR/USD moving averages assemble into proper order for an up-trend.

Source: FXtrek IntelliChart™. Copyright © 2001–2006 FXtrek.com, Inc.

Again, we'll look to the daily chart of EUR/USD (Figure 4.7). On the left side, the moving averages are mostly flat and jumbled in no particular order, while on the right side of the chart the moving averages assemble themselves into the correct order for an uptrend. Note that the shorter duration (10-day and 20-day) moving averages are slanting diagonally on the right side of the chart.

The spaghetti-like condition on the left side of the chart indicates that the pair is range-bound, and therefore only range-bound techniques would be used during that time. When the moving averages assemble themselves into the proper order, and the shorter moving averages begin to move diagonally instead of sideways, the currency pair now has a clear directional bias. The trader switches from range-bound techniques to trending techniques.

On the left (range-bound) side of the chart, it would be acceptable to go long at support and sell short at resistance. This is not the case on the right side of the chart; once the pair has chosen a direction, the trader should trade in that direction only. The trader would accept only long trades and would reject short trades.

Thus, the trader is assured of trading with the trend and avoids trades that move in the direction opposite the trend. Fighting a trend is a fool's errand, and is not recommended in any trading market, especially one that trends as strongly as the forex market.

FIBONACCI TECHNIQUES

No overview of forex technical analysis would be complete without a discussion of Fibonacci techniques. As you may know, Fibonacci was a famous Italian mathematician who is credited with several major innovations, including the discovery of a numeric sequence that is found throughout all of nature. Fibonacci ratios are found in everything from architecture to music to geometry. They can be seen in the number of petals growing on a flower, or the manner in which leaves grow on a tree.

The Fibonacci ratio of 61.8 percent, along with its inversion of 38.2 percent ($100 - 61.8 = 38.2$) and the point halfway between 61.8 and 38.2 (50 percent) are considered important support and resistance levels. Traders who use Fibonacci believe that after a significant directional move, the exchange rate will retrace in an amount equal to a Fibonacci ratio, most commonly 38.2 percent, 50 percent, or 61.8 percent.

While this type of technique is less popular in equities and commodities trading, it is part of the forex culture and is widely used by banks, institutional traders, and hedge funds, as well as individual currency traders. Because of its wide acceptance in forex trading, Fibonacci techniques create a kind of self-fulfilling prophecy.

In Figure 4.8, the USD/CAD currency pair is locked in a steep downtrend. The pair then rises until it encounters resistance at the 38.2 percent retracement of the downtrend.

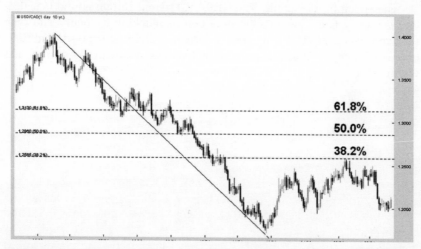

FIGURE 4.8 USD/CAD downtrend retraces 38.2 percent to Fibonacci resistance, then falls.

Source: FXtrek IntelliChart™. Copyright © 2001–2006 FXtrek.com, Inc.

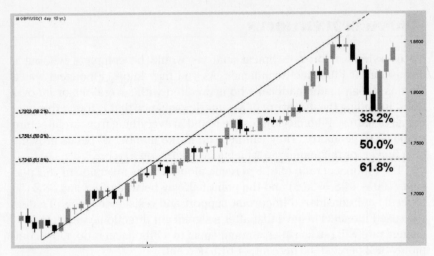

FIGURE 4.9 GBP/USD uptrend retraces 38.2 percent to Fibonacci support, and then bounces.

Source: FXtrek IntelliChart™. Copyright © 2001–2006 FXtrek.com, Inc.

Is this a coincidence? Please understand that I am a skeptic by nature, but the fact is, since I began trading forex and using Fibonacci, I've found it to be uncannily accurate for predicting major support and resistance levels in currency pairs.

Here's another example: The GBP/USD (Great Britain pound/U.S. dollar) currency pair climbs 2,000 pips before reaching its peak. The pair then retraces exactly 38.2 percent before encountering support, and then bounces higher by more than 400 pips over the next three sessions (see Figure 4.9).

CHAPTER 5

Things You Need to Know Before Trading Forex

I n the game of baseball, there are players who win games for their team through sheer speed. Often referred to as "speed demons," they intimidate opponents with their talent for stealing bases and scoring runs. Other players are known for their ability to knock the ball out of the park. Known as "power hitters," these players have the ability to shift the momentum of a game with a single swing of the bat. Another group of players is known for their defensive prowess. Their talent for negating the other team's offense by making spectacular fielding plays earns them the title of "golden glove."

Many players are proficient in one of these areas, but only the truly elite are strong in all three. That rare player who masters all of the major aspects of the sport of baseball is called a "triple threat" player.

THE "TRIPLE THREAT" TRADER

In the world of forex, the trader who masters technical analysis and trading strategies can locate profitable entry and exit points. The individual who masters fundamental analysis can anticipate turning points in the markets when economies shift. The trader who understands solid risk management can protect and defend the account against loss in any trading environment.

The trader who masters all three—technical analysis, fundamental analysis, and risk management—is truly a "triple threat" trader.

It's my sincere wish to help you become the best trader that you possibly can. You can accomplish this by mastering the three most important aspects of trading.

First, learn real techniques, in detail, that can be used to successfully trade this market. That is the purpose of this book. Learn to identify the current market situation, apply the appropriate trading strategies, and adapt to changes in the market.

Then, learn all that you can about the fundamental aspects of forex. Do not be intimidated by fundamental analysis! A solid understanding of fundamentals is often what separates the good traders from the great ones.

The third ingredient is risk management, which is the one element that all successful traders share. Good risk management will keep you out of trouble and allow you to survive the tough times and gain valuable experience.

> While the focus of this book is on technical trading strategies, don't neglect the other aspects of trading. For a well-rounded dose of all three—technical, fundamental, and risk management—please refer to my DVD series, *FXEducator—Forex Trading with Ed Ponsi*.

GAINING EXPERIENCE

Which driver is more likely to get into an accident—an experienced driver who has "seen it all" or a teenager who isn't quite sure which pedal is the accelerator and which is the brake?

Of course, the answer is the latter. A new driver is an accident waiting to happen, while an experienced driver can anticipate problems before they occur. In driving and in trading, there is no substitute for experience.

A good trading education can teach you many things, but it can't give you experience. Luckily, anyone can gain experience trading the forex market without risking hard-earned money, by using a practice or "demo" account. Most forex market makers offer these accounts, which often include real-time charts, price quotes, and news feeds.

I wish we'd them back when I got started! In the "old days," traders had to learn—and make mistakes—with real money. One of the offices where I worked had an early version of a practice account called a "trading simulator," but it wasn't comparable to the demo programs that are available today.

Demo trading is a great way for potential forex traders to familiarize themselves with this market. I highly recommend that every trader use a demo account for *at least* several months before making an attempt at live trading. If you are already trading with real money, don't be afraid to revert to a demo account if you hit a rough patch.

"Mini" accounts are also available, so that forex neophytes can place live trades with minimal risk. These mini accounts can be opened with as little as a few hundred dollars, creating one of the lowest barriers to entry for any trading market.

Trade a demo account successfully for at least several months before advancing to a mini account. Successful trading is not the same as luck; if you turn a profit in the demo, but incur excessive risk in the process, that would not be sufficient to graduate to live trading.

Once you've gained experience, traded successfully, and entered your "comfort zone," try opening a mini account. If you can trade successfully in the mini account for several months, without taking outsized risks, you might consider opening a full-sized account.

Don't rush this process; if you're uncomfortable at any point along the way, you're not ready to graduate to the next step. Take your time; the market will still be there when you're ready.

Remember, until you gain sufficient experience, you're just like that kid behind the wheel of his dad's car—an accident waiting to happen.

WHICH PAIR TO TRADE?

When you first begin to trade forex, you should start with just one currency pair. The best way to begin is with a pair that has a narrow spread, such as the EUR/USD pair. The spread is the difference between the buy price and the sell price for the currency pair.

The spread is a formidable opponent, and pairs that have wide spreads are suited only to long-term trading. Once you have overcome the spread, you have reached the "break-even" point of the trade. This is easier to achieve when the spread is narrow.

Start with EUR/USD (in a demo account, of course), and when you feel comfortable with the way the pair moves, then branch out and try GBP/USD. You'll find that this pair trades in a similar fashion to EUR/USD, but with greater volatility. Some traders enjoy this added volatility, while others can't stand it.

Since no two traders are exactly alike, it's up to you to decide which pairs suit your personal style. Any time that you are testing a new currency pair or trading technique, be sure to do so in a demo account. Figuring out which currency pairs are the best for your personality is part of the learning process of becoming a forex trader.

Once you grow used to the movements in these two pairs, give USD/JPY and USD/CAD a try. You'll see that these two currency pairs move in a completely different manner from EUR/USD and GBP/USD. The Japanese yen pairs have their own "personalities" and are more likely to find support/resistance at round numbers.

If you enjoy trading the USD/JPY currency pair, try EUR/JPY. This pair is similar to USD/JPY, but the moves tend to be quicker, with greater volatility.

COMMODITY CURRENCIES

Next, see if USD/CAD is a pair that you enjoy trading. This has been one of my favorites because of its persistent long-term trend. The relationship between this currency pair and the price of oil is strong, as the Canadian dollar often gains ground as energy prices rise, and falls when energy prices weaken. Currencies that share a strong relationship with the price of a commodity, such as oil, are called "commodity currencies" (see Figure 5.1).

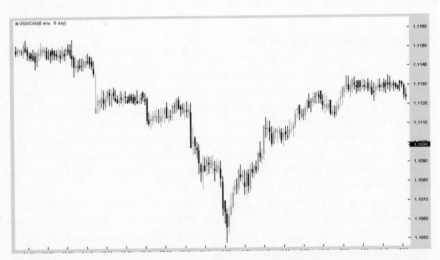

FIGURE 5.1 This wicked intraday reversal on the five-minute chart of USD/CAD coincided with the weekly release of the U.S. Department of Energy's inventory report. The report ignited volatility in the price of oil, which was reflected in the USD/CAD pair.

Source: FXtrek IntelliChart™. Copyright © 2001–2006 FXtrek.com, Inc.

FIGURE 5.2 On the weekly chart, the CAD/JPY pair rallies and then consolidates along with the price of oil in 2005–2006.

Source: FXtrek IntelliChart™. Copyright © 2001–2006 FXtrek.com, Inc.

If you want to trade a currency pair that has an even stronger relationship to the price of oil, then try Canadian dollar/Japanese yen (CAD/JPY). Canada and Japan are at opposite ends of the spectrum regarding the production and consumption of oil, and this is reflected in the CAD/JPY exchange rate (see Figure 5.2).

Canada is a major producer and exporter of oil, so the Canadian dollar benefits from higher energy costs. This is in sharp contrast with Japan, which imports nearly all of the oil it consumes. Because of this, the yen is hit hard by rising energy prices.

Another pair that enjoys a strong relationship with a commodity is AUD/USD. The Australian dollar often rises and falls along with the price of gold. This correlation can be extremely valuable to currency traders, who frequently see situations where the price of gold appears to lead the Australian dollar (see Figure 5.3).

DON'T LIMIT YOURSELF

As stated earlier, new traders should start out with one currency pair and branch out from there. However, some traders, even experienced ones, trade the same currency pair day in and day out, regardless of market conditions.

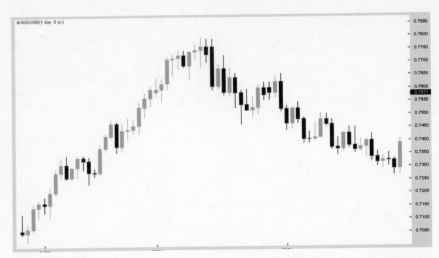

FIGURE 5.3 AUD/USD rallies along with the price of gold in the spring of 2006. After reaching a near simultaneous peak, both gold and AUD/USD pull back in tandem.

Source: FXtrek IntelliChart™. Copyright © 2001–2006 FXtrek.com, Inc.

If this works for your style of trading, that's fine, but consider that not every currency pair is always setting up for a good trade. Every pair goes through phases when it has a clear direction and is relatively easy to trade, and other times when trading that pair is considerably more difficult. When you consider this fact, it really doesn't make sense to limit yourself to one pair.

Think of it this way: Imagine that you have a garage full of autos, and you have a wide range of different choices as to which car you can drive at any time. On a day when you want to cruise the autobahn, you could drive the Porsche or the Ferrari. If you want to drive off-road, you might choose the Jeep or the Land Rover. Your choice would reflect current conditions—you probably wouldn't drive a convertible in the rain!

What would you think of someone in this situation who chooses to drive the same vehicle every day, regardless of the situation? This person has a garage full of vehicles, yet he always drives the same car, no matter if it is raining or snowing, or if the sun is shining. He even drives it when the tires are flat!

The different currency pairs are just like the cars in that garage. Sure, when you first learn how to drive, you should drive the same car all the time, so that you can establish a familiarity with that particular vehicle and concentrate on the task at hand. Once you've learned how to drive, you would vary your choice of vehicle based on the situation.

Trading is the same way; we want to use the vehicle that best suits the situation. If one currency pair shows a persistent trend and is relatively easy to trade, we would choose that over a second pair, if the latter were trading in a random and aimless fashion.

Eventually, our chosen currency pair will cease trending, and we will have to change our tactics or use a different currency pair. In short, we'll trade the pair that offers the best trading opportunities at that time.

TRADING AND KARMA

It's been said that there is no better place to observe human behavior than on a trading desk. When I first worked in that environment in New York, I heard a comment that I found perplexing. A relatively new trader had entered the room, strutting and boasting openly and loudly of his recent successes.

"I did it again! Making money and acting funny! I am on fire, baby! I am *the man!*"

The trader went on and on about how he was "always right on target" and just couldn't seem to lose.

Shaking his head at this garish display, an experienced trader seated nearby turned to the person at the next desk and said, "The market gods will not approve of this."

Although I didn't understand at the time, his meaning soon became clear: The markets have a tendency to humble those who become too proud, and the bragging trader was tempting fate by openly reveling in his recent success. Traders who are successful over the long term rarely allow their victories to go to their heads, because in trading and in everyday life, pride often precedes a fall. Consider it a sort of "market karma" that keeps traders in line when they become too full of themselves.

In fact, in the professional environment, traders who are performing exceptionally well are often asked to rein in their trading. The risk management department of a trading desk understands, through years of experience spent observing traders, that often our greatest victories are followed by our worst defeats.

Is there really an outside force that controls the fates of traders? Are the market gods quietly observing, waiting for traders to slip up and violate some code of conduct?

No, traders sabotage themselves when they lose perspective. Successful traders sometimes become overconfident, and then move away from the very elements that gave them success in the first place. The market gods—or karma, or yin and yang, whatever you want to call it—are really just an expression, a personification of this tendency toward self-sabotage.

Respect the market in the same way that a sailor respects the sea. Like an ocean, think of the market as a vast force of nature that can be navigated but cannot be dominated. Keep your head on straight when you're trading well, and fight the urge to declare victory over the market.

SCHADENFREUDE

Winning traders are not the only ones who should fear the wrath of the market gods. Since trading occurs in a highly competitive environment, you'll find that if you are doing well, sometimes other traders will be resentful of your success and root for you to fail.

I'll never forget one particularly rough stretch, when two other traders who I thought were my friends were unable to contain their glee at my recent losing streak. Prior to this lapse, I had been "tearing it up" and I guess my good fortune had rubbed them the wrong way.

Did I get carried away while I was winning, and was I therefore "asking for it" when things went awry? Did I offend the market gods? Perhaps, but now I was paying the price. Now that the shoe was on the other foot, these two were smiling in my face like five-year-old children on Christmas morning.

The Germans have a word for this—*schadenfreude*, which loosely translates to "pleasure taken from someone else's misfortune."

Just as the market gods will deflate an egotistical trader, they also have disdain for those who revel in the losses of others. Don't indulge in *schadenfreude*, or you may find yourself working in a restaurant or teaching high school—the fates that befell my two so-called friends. If you root for the guy next to you to fail, you are likely to fail as well.

PART II

Trading Strategies for Trending Markets

This market is a force of nature. It forms massive, powerful trends that can continue on for years. It creates patterns that are as persistent as waves crashing on a beach. How do currency traders use these trends and patterns to make money in the forex market?

CHAPTER 6

Understanding Trends and Tendencies

When you drive your car, do you always use the exact same driving technique? Do you always drive precisely the same way, whether you're in heavy city traffic or on an empty six-lane highway?

Of course not. You use various driving styles at different times. If you attempted to drive through gridlocked midtown Manhattan traffic as if you were on the New Jersey Turnpike, the results would be disastrous, to say the least! When we vary our driving styles, we recognize that certain techniques are appropriate some of the time, but not all of the time. We use the right technique for the right situation.

Trading is similar in that there is no one technique that will work all the time, under any conditions. Just like the driver in our example, we must vary our trading style so that we're using the appropriate technique at the appropriate time.

TRADING CONDITIONS

There are three basic types of trading conditions:

1. *Trending* currency pairs have a definite direction (Figure 6.1).
2. *Range-bound* currency pairs bounce between support and resistance levels (Figure 6.2).
3. *Consolidating* currency pairs are trapped in a narrow, tightening area (Figure 6.3).

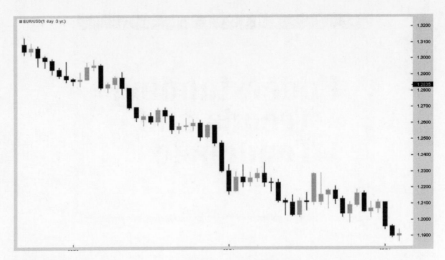

FIGURE 6.1 EUR/USD currency pair in a downtrend on the daily chart.

Source: FXtrek IntelliChart™. Copyright © 2001–2006 FXtrek.com, Inc.

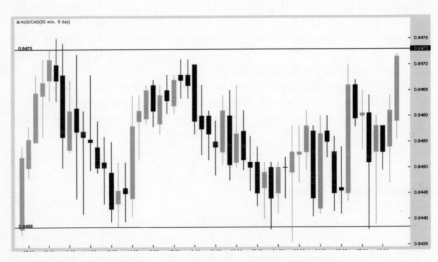

FIGURE 6.2 AUD/CAD is trapped in a range on an intraday chart.

Source: FXtrek IntelliChart™. Copyright © 2001–2006 FXtrek.com, Inc.

FIGURE 6.3 USD/JPY consolidates into an ascending triangle on the daily chart.

Source: FXtrek IntelliChart™. Copyright © 2001–2006 FXtrek.com, Inc.

Traders must approach each situation with the proper technique. Trending techniques are inappropriate during range-bound or consolidating markets, and range-bound styles will not work during trending or consolidation periods.

Here is the one thing that you must realize: *markets change*. A currency pair that is trending now will eventually begin trading in a range or move into a consolidation phase. Traders have to be nimble and adapt to this changing environment by using the right strategy at the right time.

THE IMPORTANCE OF MAINTAINING OBJECTIVITY

When you first begin using new trading techniques, you may be fortunate enough to experience success right from the start. Perhaps you just happened to use the right technique at the right time, and you were blessed with immediate gratification. Some new traders even become euphoric, because they feel that they have "mastered the market."

The unfortunate side effect of this initial success is that the trader then might continue to use that same trading technique, even when the market has clearly changed and the technique is no longer appropriate. Traders refer to this situation as "falling in love" with a technique, and the effects can be devastating.

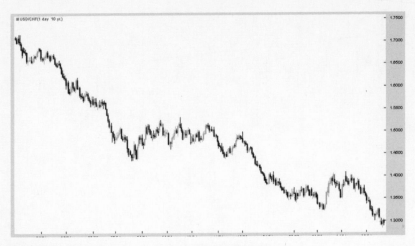

FIGURE 6.4 USD/CHF in a downtrend, 2002-2003.

Source: FXtrek IntelliChart™. Copyright © 2001-2006 FXtrek.com, Inc.

If this should happen to you, I would encourage you to try to remain objective and realize that while short-term success is not uncommon, it is not the ultimate goal. Anyone can get lucky, but luck does not always last.

For example, during the years 2002 and 2003, the U.S. dollar was falling hard against most major currencies. This created a fairly easy trading environment, as trend-following techniques worked extremely well during this time (see Figure 6.4).

Many of my students at the time were new traders who had no previous exposure to trend-following techniques. Almost immediately these "newbies" racked up huge gains by applying trend-following techniques at the appropriate time, during a trending market.

While I was happy to see my students doing well, I was concerned that they now had developed unrealistic expectations about the forex market and about trading in general. "It's not always going to be this easy," I told them. "Learn other techniques so that when the market changes, you'll be ready." Some listened, and some did not.

Sure enough, in early 2004 the U.S. dollar regained its footing, and the trend began to unravel (see Figure 6.5). Traders who realized that the trend wouldn't last forever were prepared for this change, and adjusted their tactics accordingly. Unfortunately, others had "fallen in love" with trending techniques, and continued to use them even though the situation had changed. Their results suffered as the market conditions changed.

As a trader, you don't have the luxury of falling in love with a technique, or an indicator, or a currency pair. Understand that markets are not static, and it is up to the trader to identify and adapt to these changes.

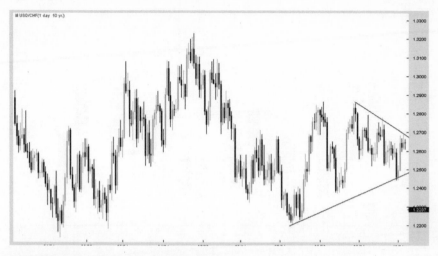

FIGURE 6.5 During the year 2004, the USD/CHF pair ceased trending. Note the consolidation triangle on the right of the chart.

Source: FXtrek IntelliChart™. Copyright © 2001–2006 FXtrek.com, Inc.

BEGIN WITH A TENDENCY

Almost every good trading strategy has at its heart a market tendency. If we observe markets for long enough, we begin to notice these tendencies; for example, the forex market tends to form long, strong trends.

Another example would be a market's tendency to find support or resistance at large round numbers, which is a psychological tendency that can occur in any trading market (see Figure 6.6). Yet another example would be the tendency for a strong breakout to occur immediately following a tight consolidation (see Figure 6.7). Any of these tendencies could be used as the basis from which to create a strategy.

A true tendency will be backed by reason; for example, round number support and resistance occur because people often locate their entries, stops, and exits right at round numbers. Why do people behave in this manner?

The fact is, not every trader consults a chart before placing a trade, and some traders have very general ideas about where they wish to place their orders. These traders often place entry, exit, and stop orders at round numbers, and their orders congregate at these levels. Because of this, round numbers often coincide with key support and resistance levels in the equity and futures markets, as well as in the forex markets.

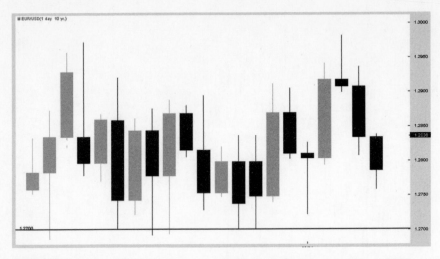

FIGURE 6.6 EUR/USD finds support repeatedly at the round number 1.2700.

Source: FXtrek IntelliChart™. Copyright © 2001–2006 FXtrek.com, Inc.

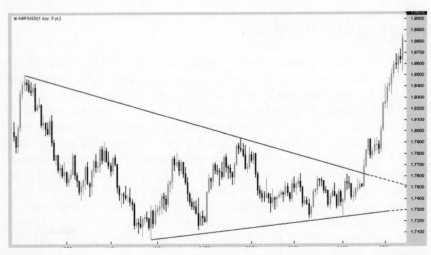

FIGURE 6.7 GBP/USD rockets out of a tight consolidation during the spring of 2006.

Source: FXtrek IntelliChart™. Copyright © 2001–2006 FXtrek.com, Inc.

Contrast this with a weak or false tendency, which is usually the result of a superficial observation. An example of a false tendency would be a statement such as, "The euro is always strong on Thursday" or "The Canadian dollar is volatile when the moon is full." Such an observation probably occurred over a short period of time and has no basis in logical reasoning. Actually, I wouldn't consider these examples to be tendencies at all; instead, I would classify them as coincidences. The odds of success when basing a trade on a weak or false tendency are the same as flipping a coin (actually worse, once you account for the spread).

PUTTING THE TREND TO WORK

Let's take a look at an example of how traders can use trends to their advantage. Consider that when a market is trending, it has chosen a clear direction. We want to assume that this trend will continue, because history tells us that in the forex market, trends can last for years. If we can get on the "right side" of the trend (long in an uptrend, or short in a downtrend), we might have an opportunity to enjoy a substantial gain.

You may have heard the phrase, "Let your winners run." This is good trading advice, as many of us have a tendency to get out of our winning trades too soon and hold on to our losing trades for too long.

It's much easier (and more profitable) to allow your winning trades to run in a trending market, because the exchange rate has a clear direction. As long as the currency pair is moving in that direction, our protective stop is less likely to be triggered.

Contrast this with a sideways or range-bound currency pair. Since this pair has no real direction, the price has a tendency to "come back" toward the entry point. This makes it more difficult for traders to hold on to their positions, and forces them to be nimble regarding exits. Sideways markets are tradable too, but this situation calls for different techniques than when the market is trending.

SELF-FULFILLING PROPHECY

Not all trends are created equal. The best trends are the ones that jump right off of the chart—one glance and you can see it and identify it immediately.

Like many aspects of technical analysis, trends that are obvious tend to work well because many traders can see and identify them. If enough traders then place orders that reflect their belief that the currency pair is trending, this provides additional fuel for the trend.

This is an example of the "self-fulfilling prophecy," a prediction that, in being made, actually causes itself to become true. In other words, if traders believe that a currency pair is in an uptrend, many of them will go long in an attempt to take advantage of the trend. The resulting buying pressure drives the pair higher, reinforcing the trend. The self-fulfilling prophecy is a recurring theme in technical analysis and in forex trading.

TAKE ME TO THE RIVER

I like to compare a trend to a current in a river. If you have ever gone white-water rafting, you might know that most rivers are rated on an ascending scale. At the low end of the scale, the current is so weak that there is little point in putting your raft into the water. As we move higher up the scale, the currents become stronger, and the "rafter" is more quickly carried toward his or her destination.

Like the rafter, the trader wants to reach a target. Using a weak trend to place a trade is likely to lead to a weak result, as the exchange rate is not as "committed" to one particular direction. A strong trend indicates strong commitment and will carry the trader farther and faster toward his or her target.

Equally important is the fact that the trader who fights against the trend will soon find that his raft is "taking on water" as he fights his way upstream. Fighting trends is a common cause of failure for prospective traders, so we must resolve that we will trade only with the trend and never against it.

Can a trend be too strong? A huge run-up in a stock, commodity, or currency can potentially lead to a steep correction. Be aware of situations where a trading instrument has already garnered massive gains. However, if a trader is using good risk management and is using stops properly, and is trading in a highly liquid environment such as the spot forex market, the amount of risk in any situation can be reduced and controlled.

(River currents *can* be too strong. If you have ever had your raft stretched like a rubber band by violent rapids, the resulting slingshot effect can launch the person in the back of the raft out of the boat and high into the air like a human missile. Care to guess how I learned this fun fact? Rafters and traders alike should use all necessary safety precautions.)

HOW TO DETERMINE IF THE MARKET IS TRENDING

There are several common techniques used to determine if a trend is in effect. One popular method involves the use of moving averages and is often referred to as the *proper order* of moving averages, which was discussed in an earlier chapter.

Another way to determine if a currency pair is trending is by using the average directional index (ADX) indicator. The ADX indicator, created by the prolific J. Welles Wilder, indicates the strength of the trend without regard to the direction of the trend (upward or downward). High readings indicate strong trends; for example, the ADX indicator's giving a reading above 35 and rising would be an indication of a strongly trending market (see Figure 6.8).

Yet another way to determine if the market is trending is through the use of trend lines. A trend line is simply a line that is drawn beneath an uptrend, or above a downtrend, and indicates the general direction of a currency pair (see Figure 6.9).

Be careful when it comes to using trend lines to determine exact points of support and resistance, because they are subjective in nature. If you ask

FIGURE 6.8 ADX indicator gives a reading above 35 and rising, indicating a strong trend.

Source: FXtrek IntelliChart™. Copyright © 2001–2006 FXtrek.com, Inc.

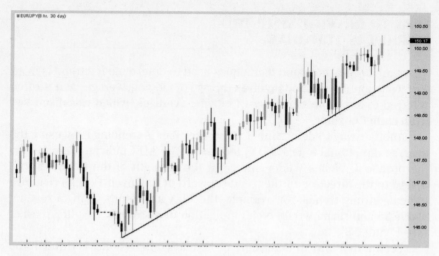

FIGURE 6.9 Trend line indicates EUR/JPY is in a persistent uptrend, summer of 2006.

Source: FXtrek IntelliChart™. Copyright © 2001–2006 FXtrek.com, Inc.

10 different traders to draw a trend line on a chart, you might end up with 10 different trend lines. Because we are all drawing slightly different trend lines, we will all have slightly different entry and exit points. The concept of a "soft target" applies to trend lines as well as other types of support and resistance.

CHAPTER 7

The Anatomy of a Trend

Perhaps you have heard the saying, "The trend is your friend." This is one of the oldest sayings on Wall Street, and there is good reason for its popularity. Trading with the trend is one of the most profitable and time-honored methods used to trade any market, but it is particularly effective when trading the forex market. This is because the forex market has a tendency to form strong trends that can last for weeks, months, or even years.

Why are forex trends so much stronger and longer lasting than trends in other markets? Consider the differences between trends in the equity market versus trends in the forex market.

In the equity market, if a stock is performing poorly, there is a certain set of actions that can be taken to remedy the situation. For example, the company can be restructured, or the chief executive officer can be replaced. These actions can cause a rapid change in the fundamental outlook of the company, which will sooner or later be reflected in the price of the stock. This process can happen quickly, sometimes in just a couple of months.

WHY TRENDS FORM

Consider that when we trade in the forex market, we are trading the economies of entire nations. As you may know, when a country's economy is strong or weak, it often remains that way for years. You can't simply boost the economy of an entire nation by replacing its leader or by performing a few accounting tricks.

Economic strength and weakness runs in a cycle that is measured in years. Traditional business cycles undergo four stages: expansion, prosperity, contraction, and recession. Economic indicators such as gross domestic product (GDP), which measures the size and growth rate of an economy, measure these fluctuations.

Periods of growth often end with the failure of speculative investments, which are built on a bubble of confidence that bursts or deflates. After a recessionary phase, the economy gathers momentum, allowing the expansionary phase to begin again.

The perceived economic strength or weakness of an economy is usually reflected in the underlying currency. Since Forex trading involves matching two currencies against one another, situations often arise in which one currency is much stronger than the other currency in the pair. The result is a trend that can last for months or years, much to the delight of traders who use trend-following techniques.

One example of this phenomenon is the relationship between the U.S. dollar and the Japanese yen. In late 2005, this currency pair, represented by the symbol USD/JPY, had been trending higher for several months, as reflected in Figure 7.1.

The year 2005 was a banner year for the U.S. dollar, as an economic recovery led to strong growth. Because U.S. growth was so strong, the Federal Reserve, which is the central bank that makes monetary policy

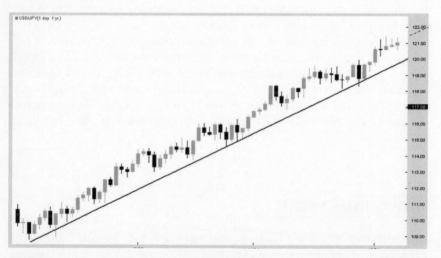

FIGURE 7.1 Fundamental factors drove the uptrend in USD/JPY in late 2005.

Source: FXtrek IntelliChart™. Copyright © 2001–2006 FXtrek.com, Inc.

decisions for the nation, embarked on a campaign of interest rate increases, in an effort to slow economic growth to a sustainable pace. This underlying strength was reflected in the U.S. dollar, which showed considerable gains versus the euro (Figure 7.2), the British pound (Figure 7.3), and the Japanese yen in 2005.

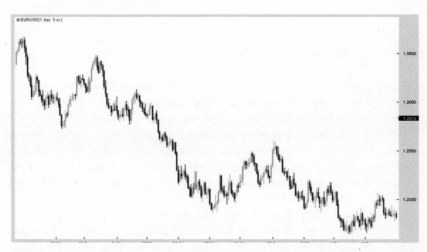

FIGURE 7.2 A strong economy boosts the U.S. dollar against the euro in 2005, causing the EUR/USD pair to fall.

Source: FXtrek IntelliChart™. Copyright © 2001–2006 FXtrek.com, Inc.

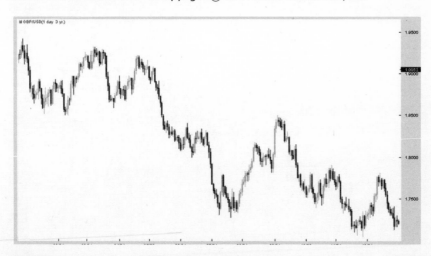

FIGURE 7.3 U.S. dollar gains against the British pound in 2005, causing a decline in the GBP/USD pair.

Source: FXtrek IntelliChart™. Copyright © 2001–2006 FXtrek.com, Inc.

Meanwhile, Japan's interest rates hovered close to zero, with no chance for an increase in the near future. Japan had revised downward its economic growth data for the year 2005, saying that GDP grew at just 1.7 percent. This represents a decrease from the previous year's growth of 2.3 percent. Considering the diverging fortunes of these two countries, the conditions were ripe for a trending scenario.

DON'T FIGHT THE TREND

The first credo of the trend-following trader is, "Don't fight the trend." It is very tempting to try to guess the point at which the trend will reverse, but this is exactly what we want to avoid doing.

This is just human nature; it is much easier for us as human beings to imagine the price returning to a level that is still fresh in our recent memory, as opposed to imagining the price rising to levels that have not been seen in years. Yet that is exactly what happened in the USD/JPY trend.

There is one thing of which you can be certain: During any trend, there are numerous traders who are attempting to fight against the trend, and the majority of them are losing money. While it is possible to turn a profit on a countertrend move, the trader who consistently trades in this fashion is stacking the odds against himself and asking for trouble.

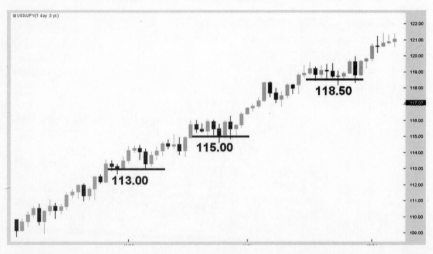

FIGURE 7.4 USD/JPY support levels form within the uptrend at round numbers.

Source: FXtrek IntelliChart™. Copyright © 2001–2006 FXtrek.com, Inc.

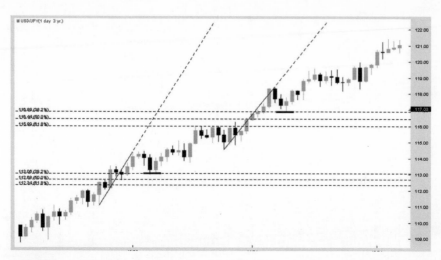

FIGURE 7.5 Fibonacci retracement levels acting as support within the USD/JPY uptrend.

Source: FXtrek IntelliChart™. Copyright © 2001–2006 FXtrek.com, Inc.

Meanwhile, the trend-following trader is searching for opportunities to go long the currency pair in an uptrend, and rejects trades that fight against the direction of the dominant trend. This trader wants to enter a long trade, but will not simply enter at a random point. Instead, he or she is seeking a pullback.

In an uptrend, this pullback can occur as the price falls back toward a prior level of support, or perhaps to a Fibonacci retracement level. Large round numbers can often act as psychological support or resistance as well, because orders tend to accumulate at these levels. In Figure 7.4, we can see three examples of support levels that formed during the uptrend. Notice that several of the levels also correspond with large round numbers.

Fibonacci can be a useful tool for determining a point of entry during an uptrend. The concept of Fibonacci is that a directional move in a market will often retrace by a certain percentage. According to Fibonacci, the most important retracement levels are 38.2 percent, 50 percent, and 61.8 percent. We can see that during the uptrend in the USD/JPY pair, there were several pullbacks to the key 38.2 percent retracement level. These pullbacks served as excellent opportunities to enter in the direction of the trend, as the price often finds support at these retracement levels (Figure 7.5).

CHAPTER 8

Forex Multiple Time Frame Strategy

Keep in mind what was said in Chapter 6 about strategy development: Every strategy begins with a tendency.

One of the most dependable features of the forex market is its tendency to form trends in a variety of time frames. Forex trends can continue for weeks, months, or even years, and traders who align themselves with these trends improve their chances of success. Let's look at some specific techniques to capitalize on this well-known forex market tendency.

Frequently when we trade, we may look at currency pair's chart and receive contradictory signals from various indicators. Which signals should we follow, and which ones should we ignore? When we are in doubt, it's helpful to look at the big picture, by moving to a longer time frame. Let's assume for our example that we are placing trades based on the hourly chart:

- First, look to the longer-term chart, which is the daily chart in this example, to see if the currency pair is trending. There are several ways to do this; simply draw a trend line, or use an indicator that is designed to determine market trend. For instance, the average directional index (ADX) indicator could be used to determine if the market is trending. Or we could look to moving averages to determine if they're in the "proper order" formation.
- Often, the trend will be obvious without the use of any trend lines or indicators. The best trends are the ones that are obvious, because other traders can see the trend and act on it, creating a "self-fulfilling prophecy."

- If the currency pair is trending higher, trade from the long side only. If it is trending lower, trade from the short side only. If there is no discernible trend, then don't attempt to place a trade using this technique, as it is specifically designed for use in trending markets.
- First, we'll determine the direction in which we want to trade from the long-term chart; then, we'll look to the short-term chart to locate our entry point, stop, and exits.
- If we have determined that we are in an uptrend on the daily chart, we can go long if the price falls to a level of support on the hourly chart. Or we can go long if an oscillator, such as relative strength index (RSI), indicates that the pair is oversold on the hourly chart. Enter long with your stop below the area of support.
- In the case of a downtrend on the daily chart, we will seek to sell at resistance on the hourly chart, or if oscillators indicate that the pair is overbought on the hourly chart.

Remember, if the daily chart is in an uptrend, we can only go long. If the daily chart is in a downtrend, we can only sell short. If we cannot tell if the market is trending, then we cannot use trending techniques such as this one.

As you will see, there are many variations on this theme. Essentially, I'm going to use everything at my disposal to locate good entry points and put my trade in harmony with the daily trend.

WHY DOES IT WORK?

This system allows us to trade only in the direction of the overall trend, and it requires that trades can be placed only after the price has pulled back to a favorable entry point. In other words, it will not allow the trader to enter long at the highs or enter short at the lows.

The technique can also be used in shorter time frames; for example, an active day trader can use a four-hour chart as the longer-term chart and a 15-minute chart as the shorter-term chart.

Take a look at this long-term trend in the U.S. dollar/Canadian dollar currency pair in Figure 8.1. As you can see, the exchange rate had been falling steadily for years, from above 1.60 in 2002 to below 1.10 in 2006.

During these years, the prices of commodities like gold and oil made spectacular gains. Canada, a major producer and exporter of energy products and metals, benefited from the increasing flow of capital that it received in payment for these goods. This is why the loonie is often referred to as a "commodity currency."

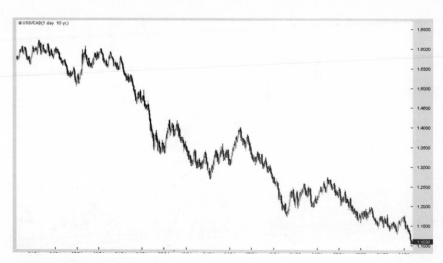

FIGURE 8.1 A long-term downtrend in USD/CAD pair.

Source: FXtrek IntelliChart™. Copyright © 2001–2006 FXtrek.com, Inc.

This increased flow of capital served to strengthen the Canadian dollar, as importers such as the United States were forced to send more of their wealth to Canada in exchange for these materials.

The trend became particularly pronounced during the spring of 2006, fueled by a fierce rally in metals like gold, silver, and copper. The rally helped to push the Canadian dollar to a 27-year high versus the greenback, and simultaneously the currency pair reached multidecade lows in early May (see Figure 8.2).

Then in mid-May, after a spectacular run, gold, propelled by massive hedge fund buying, peaked at $730 per ounce. At about the same time, the USD/CAD pair bottomed out. As profit takers emerged, gold began to float lower, and the USD/CAD pair began to drift higher (see Figure 8.3).

As trend traders, our objective is to use this trend to our advantage. Because the currency pair is in a downtrend, we will look only for short entries, and ignore any opportunity to go long. Since the pair is rallying, we need to locate our entry point. We want to locate a major resistance level.

COMBINING FIBONACCI AND TREND

Whenever a major forex trend begins to falter, traders look to Fibonacci retracements to try to determine where the trend might resume. In this case, we are looking for a point of resistance, to create a superior entry

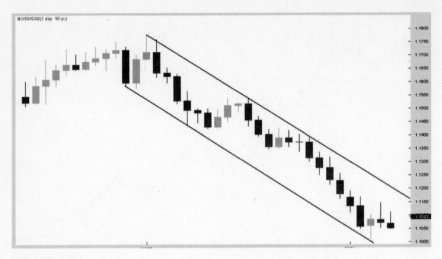

FIGURE 8.2   Commodity rally pushes USD/CAD to a new low.

Source: FXtrek IntelliChart™. Copyright © 2001–2006 FXtrek.com, Inc.

FIGURE 8.3   Pullback in gold and other commodities eases pressure on USD/CAD.

Source: FXtrek IntelliChart™. Copyright © 2001–2006 FXtrek.com, Inc.

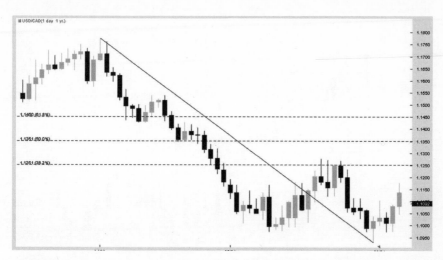

FIGURE 8.4 Fibonacci is used to locate possible entry points for a short trade.

Source: FXtrek IntelliChart™. Copyright © 2001–2006 FXtrek.com, Inc.

for our trade. We want to sell short, so that when the trend reasserts itself, we'll be trading in harmony with the trend. In this case, let's draw our Fibonacci from a peak in early April down to the low in late May (see Figure 8.4).

We can see that the 38.2 percent retracement of the recent downtrend is a possible point of entry. Additionally, this Fibonacci level coincides with the area of 1.1250, which acted as resistance several weeks earlier. We'll consider the 38.2 percent Fibonacci retracement at 1.1250 an area of resistance for now (see Figure 8.5).

Several days later, the exchange rate has reached the Fibonacci level, and the pair is trading at resistance. Should we place a trade? Not yet; instead, let's see if we can increase our chances of success. The trader looks to the hourly chart to try to locate prior resistance or an overbought oscillator, such as the RSI or the slow stochastic indicator.

In this case, we can see in Figure 8.6 that as the exchange rate approaches the vicinity of 1.1250, the RSI (calculated using 14 periods) climbs into overbought territory.

OVERBOUGHT DOES NOT EQUAL "SELL"

There is an important distinction that must be made at this point, because there are many traders who will simply sell because the pair is now in

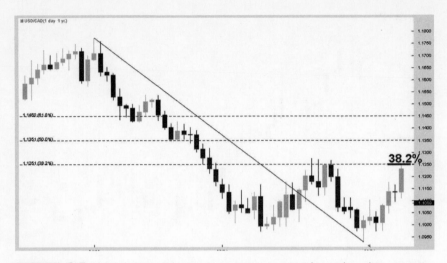

FIGURE 8.5   38.2 percent Fibonacci retracement coincides with earlier support.

Source: FXtrek IntelliChart™. Copyright © 2001–2006 FXtrek.com, Inc.

FIGURE 8.6   RSI is in overbought territory on the hourly chart.

Source: FXtrek IntelliChart™. Copyright © 2001–2006 FXtrek.com, Inc.

overbought territory. Consider this for a moment: Just because a currency pair (or a stock or a commodity) is overbought, does this mean that it cannot go higher?

Think back to some of the persistent rallies that have occurred in the markets, for example the great run of the NASDAQ at the end of the twentieth century. I'm sure that oscillators and other indicators showed that the NASDAQ was overbought, but did that stop it from going higher? How many people lost money trying to fight that trend?

If there is one phrase that makes me cringe, it's when somebody tells me, "It can't go any higher" (or, if the trading instrument is falling, "It can't go any lower"). The price or exchange rate can *always* go higher after a big rally, or lower after a huge drop, and it often does just that. As traders, we have to accept the fact that anything is possible once we have entered a trade.

How do we know for certain that the price has peaked before we can sell short? We can never know for sure, because nothing is certain in trading. Trading is just the art of stacking probabilities in our favor. Fortunately, there is a way that we can increase our chances of success.

I recommend waiting for the oscillator to drop from the overbought level and into neutral territory. This is often an early indication that the momentum is turning, and a counter move may be in the offing.

PICKING TOPS AND BOTTOMS

Certainly, if we wait for the oscillator to turn before entry, we will not enter at the absolute peak. Many traders seem to be overly concerned with getting in at the ultimate entry point. In other words, they want to sell short at the peak and go long at the absolute bottom.

The problem with picking tops and bottoms is that it is a hazardous game. Nobody can accurately predict the peaks and valleys in stocks, futures, options, or forex, and a trader who tries this is simply attempting to get lucky. It's the equivalent of a poker player's trying to draw to an inside straight; it might work some of the time, but in the long run the odds are against you.

If we wait for the momentum to turn, we have no chance of entering at the very top or bottom, but that's okay. Experienced traders are willing to sacrifice a portion of the move, in exchange for the increased probability of success that patience provides.

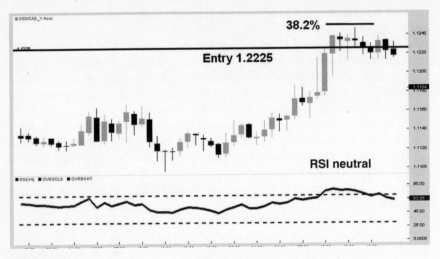

FIGURE 8.7 RSI dips from overbought to neutral, creating a short entry.

Source: FXtrek IntelliChart™. Copyright © 2001–2006 FXtrek.com, Inc.

THE ENTRY SIGNAL

As the exchange rate slides and the RSI descends from overbought levels, we prepare to enter our short trade. When the exchange rate drops, we enter short in the vicinity of 1.1225, the point at which the RSI is no longer giving an overbought reading (see Figure 8.7).

PLACING THE STOP

We must immediately enter a stop order to protect against any adverse movement. We have several options for doing this, and the first option will be to place the stop above the recent high of 1.1245.

What is the rationale for locating the stop at this point? Consider the possibility that, after our entry, the exchange rate could rally further. Do we really want to hold on to this currency pair if it changes direction and reaches a new, higher high?

No, if the pair trades above 1.1245, we don't want to hold on to it, as it could be breaking out to the upside. So, we'll place our stop in a location that will take us out of the trade if a new high is reached.

Don't forget that we also have the Fibonacci resistance point at 1.1250. Since this might give our stop added security, we want our stop to be

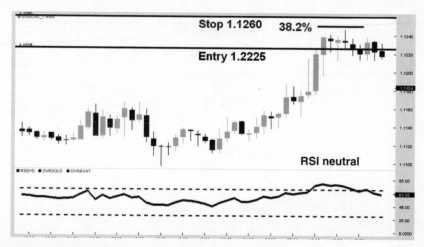

FIGURE 8.8 The stop is placed above the recent high and above the 38.2 percent Fibonacci retracement.

Source: FXtrek IntelliChart™. Copyright © 2001–2006 FXtrek.com, Inc.

located above 1.1250. This also satisfies our requirement that the stop should be located above the recent high of 1.1245. If we place the stop at 1.1260, the stop will be located above the recent high *and* above the Fibonacci level, giving our trade additional protection (see Figure 8.8).

The entry point of 1.1225, along with the stop at 1.1260, creates risk of 35 pips per lot. If this is an unacceptable degree of risk, the trade cannot be placed.

GETTING OUT

Next, we'll need to locate our exit points in order to take profit. I usually don't exit my trades all at once; instead, I like to exit my trades in portions. So, if I have entered two lots, I'll close 50 percent of the trade at each exit. If I've entered three lots, I'll exit 33 percent per exit, and so on. The number of lots entered is a function of risk management, as we'll see when we progress further. In this trade we will sell short three lots, so we'll need three exits to close the trade.

We'll create our first exit by measuring the risk of the trade, which we have already determined to be 35 pips per lot. If our trade reaches the point at which we are profitable by the amount of pips that are risked (per lot), we can then exit a portion of the trade. We need the exchange rate to fall to 1.1190 in order to generate a 35-pip profit, so 1.1190 will be our first exit point (see Figure 8.9).

FIGURE 8.9   The initial exit of 1.1190 represents a 1:1 risk-reward ratio.

Source: FXtrek IntelliChart™. Copyright © 2001–2006 FXtrek.com, Inc.

FIGURE 8.10   Prior support at the round number of 1.1100 can be used as a secondary exit.

Source: FXtrek IntelliChart™. Copyright © 2001–2006 FXtrek.com, Inc.

Next, we'll look for areas of prior support (meaning areas that the exchange rate had difficulty penetrating on earlier attempts, due to buyers stepping in at those levels). Looking back, we can see that the price bounced repeatedly from 1.1100, which is also a round number (round numbers often act as support or resistance). Let's use 1.1100 for our second exit (see Figure 8.10).

FIGURE 8.11 Prior support at 1.0975, a multidecade low at that time.

Source: FXtrek IntelliChart™. Copyright © 2001–2006 FXtrek.com, Inc.

A further look shows that the price had difficulty getting through the area of 1.0975 on several occasions. Let's designate this area for our final exit (see Figure 8.11).

WELCOME TO THE REAL WORLD

Let's take a closer look at those last two exits and think about how they can be improved. When we are trading in the real world, does the exchange rate always fall to the exact level of support, or are markets slightly more random than this?

If you've been trading in the real world, you know that the exchange rate or price rarely falls repeatedly to the exact same level of support or consistently rises to an exact level of resistance. Sometimes the price falls below the anticipated support level, and sometimes it doesn't quite make it all the way down.

This is why we say that support and resistance are "areas," not exact price points, and we need to use "soft targets" instead of assuming markets will perform to precise expectations.

TWEAKING THE EXITS

When we consider the true nature of trading and acknowledge that there is a certain degree of randomness to any trading market, it becomes

FIGURE 8.12 The second exit of 1.1100 is raised to 1.1115.

Source: FXtrek IntelliChart™. Copyright © 2001–2006 FXtrek.com, Inc.

necessary to adjust our exits. Instead of expecting the exchange rate to cooperate and reach the "bottom" of support at exactly 1.1100, let's tweak this exit to improve our chances of success.

According to the daily chart, major resistance is located at 1.1250, based on the 38.2 percent Fibonacci retracement that we discussed earlier. Since a support level is located at 1.1100, this would constitute a 150-pip range from support to resistance (1.1250 − 1.1100 = 150).

Let's raise our exit by an amount equivalent to 10% of that range, which would be 15 pips (10% of 150 pips). This pushes our second exit higher, from 1.1100 to 1.1115. (see Figure 8.12).

This has the dual effect of placing our exit in a location where it is more likely to be reached, above the very bottom of support, and it also allows us to exit ahead of the round number of 1.1100. Round numbers often act as psychological support or resistance levels, because orders tend to accumulate at these points.

There is still the matter of our final exit, currently located at 1.0975. If we apply the same technique to improving this exit, we would first measure the distance from support to resistance, which is approximately 275 pips (1.1250 − 1.0975 = 275).

Ten percent of 275 is equal to 27.5 pips (we'll round it up to 28), so let's raise this exit by 28 pips, to 1.1003. Again, this will raise the exit to an area that is more likely to be reached, since it's in the middle of the support

FIGURE 8.13   Third exit is raised above round number support of 1.1000.

Source: FXtrek IntelliChart™. Copyright © 2001–2006 FXtrek.com, Inc.

area instead of at the very bottom of support. It also raises our stop above a huge psychological support level, the round number of 1.1000 (see Figure 8.13).

Because the first exit at 1.1190 is not based on support or resistance, but instead is a function of the amount of risk taken on the trade, this exit will remain unchanged.

EXECUTING THE PLAN

If the exchange rate moves in our favor and reaches 1.1190, we'll exit a portion of the trade (in this case one lot, or one-third of the trade) and lower our stop to the entry point. In other words, when the exchange rate reaches 1.1190, the plan is to cover one lot and move the stop on the remaining two lots to 1.1225.

This will have the dual effect of locking in a small profit and eliminating the remaining risk from the trade. Remember, amateurs are concerned with how much they can make, while professionals are concerned with how much they can lose. Let's trade like professionals and keep risk at the forefront of our concerns.

Once our stop has been lowered to the break-even point, our worst-case scenario consists of a 35-pip gain on the first lot and breaking even on

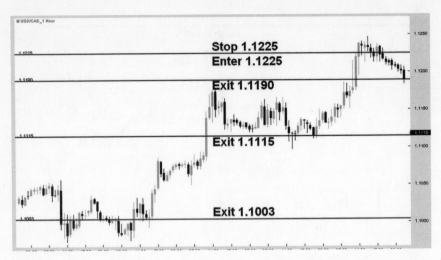

FIGURE 8.14 The first exit is reached; take a partial profit and lower the stop to 1.1225.

Source: FXtrek IntelliChart™. Copyright © 2001–2006 FXtrek.com, Inc.

the second and third lot. Now we have assured ourselves of at least a small gain, with the possibility of additional gains, all while having eliminated the risk (see Figure 8.14).

SECOND-GUESSING

At this point, it would not be unusual if the exchange rate were to rise and reach our stop, leaving the trader with a small gain. If this were to happen, would it mean that something had been done incorrectly or that this was a "bad trade"?

What if the price rises, takes out the stop, and then begins falling? Does that mean that there is something wrong with this technique?

These thoughts are a type of second-guessing that is natural when things don't go exactly according to plan. When confronted with these thoughts, it's important to learn to trust our trading plan and refrain from this type of behavior.

We can't control the outcome of any individual trade, and markets do not always cooperate as we wish they would. It is possible to execute a plan perfectly and still lose money on a trade. However, if we create good plans and execute them properly on a consistent basis, we will be miles ahead of most traders.

BRINGING IT HOME

Fortunately, in this case, the massive downtrend kicks in, and a sharp move lower ensues. Now the exchange rate has reached our second exit, and it's time to cover another lot, this time at 1.1115. We'll "celebrate" by lowering our stop again, from its current location of 1.1225 to the former location of the first exit, at 1.1190 (see Figure 8.15).

Since we are more concerned with losses than gains, we will once again consider our worst-case scenario. We have now locked in a profit of 35 pips on the first lot and 110 pips on the second lot. At worst, the exchange rate will rise to 1.1190, taking us out of our third lot for a 35-pip profit. Not bad for a worst-case scenario!

After drifting sideways for a while, the trading gods smile upon us as the exchange rate finally dives to reach our last exit point at 1.1003 (see Figure 8.16). The trade concludes with a profit of 35 pips on the first lot, a profit of 110 pips on the second lot, and a profit of 222 pips on the third lot. Good things happen when we trade with the trend!

THE DEVIL'S ADVOCATE

But wait! I can hear the nagging voice of that devil's advocate once again, saying, "You shouldn't have raised those exits! If you had just left them

FIGURE 8.15 The second exit is reached; the stop is lowered to the former location of the first exit, 1.1190.

Source: FXtrek IntelliChart™. Copyright © 2001–2006 FXtrek.com, Inc.

FIGURE 8.16 The USD/CAD exchange rate plummets to the third exit.

Source: FXtrek IntelliChart™. Copyright © 2001–2006 FXtrek.com, Inc.

where they were, at 1.1100 and 1.0975, the exits still would have been reached, and you would have earned more pips!"

In this case, it's true that the original exits were reached. Does that mean it was wrong to raise the exits? Should we change our strategy so that next time we will not adjust the exits?

Absolutely not! The outcome of any one individual trade is not important, what matters is the outcome over a large sample of trades. If we were to change our approach every time things didn't go exactly according to plan, we would be in a constant state of adjusting our strategies.

In fact, we would not be following a trading strategy at all! Instead, we would exist in a perpetual state of second-guessing. To avoid this fate, all we have to do is plan our trade and then execute our plan. If we are following a good trading plan, we will be pleased with the overall result, despite the outcome of any individual trade.

As we can see in Figure 8.17, the trade fell right to the bottom of support, and then the currency pair began to bounce higher.

WHEN TO STAY OUT

Since the pair is rising up from support, should we enter a long trade and try to profit from a possible bounce? The answer is no. If you recall, the original plan was to trade only in the direction of the trend and to reject trades that go against the trend.

FIGURE 8.17 USD/CAD bounces up from 1.0975, a major support area.

Source: FXtrek IntelliChart™. Copyright © 2001–2006 FXtrek.com, Inc.

Does this mean that trades that go against the trend are never profitable? No, anything can happen in an individual trade. In this case, we see that a trader who fought the downtrend in USD/CAD would have profited, but it is only one trade. A trader who fights against the trend on a consistent basis will have a difficult time finding success.

When a trader who uses this strategy properly sees the exchange rate rising, he or she is not tempted to go long and battle against the odds. The proper trading attitude would be to allow the exchange rate to rise, and hope that it creates another short entry opportunity. As we will see, this is exactly what happened, as the exchange rate climbed once more to the Fibonacci level of 1.1250.

RELOADING THE TRADE

As the exchange rate rises back to 1.1250, the RSI indicator drifts into overbought levels. The RSI then dives back into neutral territory, creating a new entry in harmony with the downtrend (see Figure 8.18).

Now we have another opportunity to capitalize on the downtrend. In this case, all of the calculations that were used to create the previous trade are still valid (support and resistance have not changed), so we can use the same entry, stop, and exits that were used earlier (see Figure 8.19).

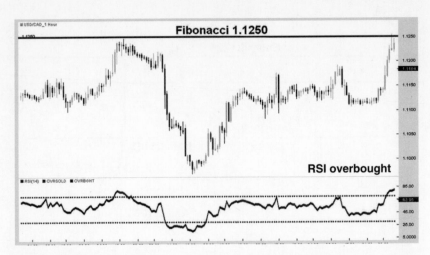

FIGURE 8.18   RSI is overbought as the USD/CAD pair reaches resistance again.

Source: FXtrek IntelliChart™. Copyright © 2001–2006 FXtrek.com, Inc.

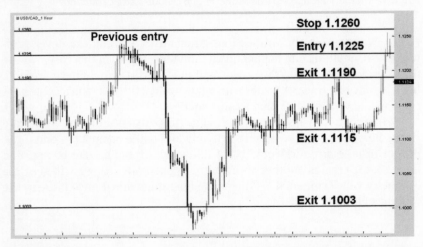

FIGURE 8.19   In this case, the same support levels from the previous trade are still applicable.

Source: FXtrek IntelliChart™. Copyright © 2001–2006 FXtrek.com, Inc.

After the trade is entered, the exchange rate drifts sideways for hours, and our stop is nearly reached on several occasions. Finally, the price hits 1.1190 and we are able to take a partial profit (see Figure 8.20).

Just as we exit a portion of the trade for a 35-pip profit, we lower the stop from 1.1260 to the entry point of 1.1225, thereby eliminating any further risk from the trade. Now our worst-case scenario is a 35-pip profit on

FIGURE 8.20 The initial profit is taken as the first exit is reached.

Source: FXtrek IntelliChart™. Copyright © 2001–2006 FXtrek.com, Inc.

the first lot, and a break-even trade on lots two and three. Sound familiar? See Figure 8.21.

What happens next? The currency pair begins to rise and finally reaches our lowered stop (see Figure 8.22).

FANTASY VERSUS REALITY

Often, this is where the mind begins to fill with doubts and second thoughts. For example, what would have happened if we had just left the stop at 1.1260?

Again, we will not allow this type of thinking. Many traders are looking for a "holy grail" technique that will allow them to win all the time. Remember the "pleasure principle"; we want to win all the time because winning feels good.

Unscrupulous salesmen understand this, and will try to entice you with tales of strategies that "win" 85 percent, 90 percent, or 95 percent of the time. Unfortunately, there is no such thing as a "holy grail" strategy, and the sooner we stop looking for it, the sooner we can focus on becoming a successful trader in the real world.

The second trade was just as good as the first; it was only the result that varied. We cannot control the result of any one trade; we can only control our plan and execute it to the best of our ability. Thanks to the use of good

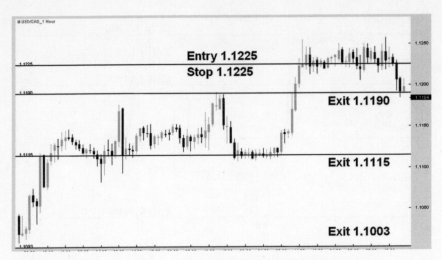

FIGURE 8.21 The stop is lowered to the entry point, eliminating further risk.

Source: FXtrek IntelliChart™. Copyright © 2001–2006 FXtrek.com, Inc.

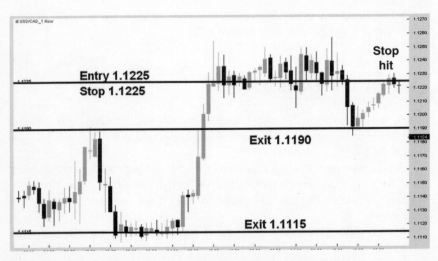

FIGURE 8.22 The stop is triggered at the entry point of 1.1225.

Source: FXtrek IntelliChart™. Copyright © 2001–2006 FXtrek.com, Inc.

risk management, we did manage to turn a small profit on the second trade, and now we can focus on the next opportunity.

PHANTOM SIGNAL

Once again, the pair rises toward the Fibonacci resistance level of 1.1250. However, not only does the exchange rate fail to reach resistance, but at the same time, the RSI fails to rise up to overbought levels. A proper sell signal has not been given, but the undisciplined trader will be tempted to enter the trade anyway (see Figure 8.23).

In this case, the undisciplined trader who entered despite the lack of a proper sell signal was rewarded, as the exchange rate plunged from the resistance area again (see Figure 8.24).

TEMPORARY SUCCESS AND FAILURE

Does this mean that we should now ignore our rules? Of course not; the undisciplined trader will win this time, but this lack of discipline will eventually cost the trader much more than what was gained here.

Soon, he or she will begin to bend and break other rules, and after a while this individual will no longer be following a cogent plan. If it's okay

FIGURE 8.23 The exchange rate fails to reach support, and RSI fails to reach overbought levels.

Source: FXtrek IntelliChart™. Copyright © 2001–2006 FXtrek.com, Inc.

FIGURE 8.24 Despite the lack of a proper signal, the exchange rate plummets.

Source: FXtrek IntelliChart™. Copyright © 2001–2006 FXtrek.com, Inc.

to enter the trade without waiting for a correct sell signal, soon it might be okay to trade without a stop. Eventually, a lack of discipline could cost this trader his or her account.

The market has a funny way of temporarily rewarding us for doing the wrong thing. We may even get away with doing the wrong thing for so long that we begin to believe that we are doing the right thing. We have to ask ourselves this question:

> *Would I rather have temporary success that is setting me up for a long-term failure, or would I rather have temporary failure that is setting me up for long-term success?*

The Fear of Missing Out

This is not to imply that there was any failure on the part of the trader who maintained discipline and stayed out of the trade. Always remember, *do not worry about the trades you do not enter; focus instead on the trades that you do enter.*

Undue concern about missed trades implies that there are a finite number of trading opportunities, and this is simply not the case. There will always be other trading opportunities, and if we are focused on what might have been, there is a chance that we might miss a great trade that is setting up right now.

THE STOP RUN

Getting back to the USD/CAD currency pair, by this time we have seen the exchange rate rejected numerous times at the 1.1250 Fibonacci resistance level. Clearly, sellers are stepping in at this level and using it as an entry point in anticipation of a resumption of the downtrend (see Figure 8.25).

By now, the resistance level has become fairly obvious, so we can assume that there are many traders, both individual and institutional, selling short in the vicinity of 1.1250. We have to ask ourselves, where are these traders placing their stops? Most likely, the stops are located above resistance. If there is a large amount of selling at this level, then logic dictates that there must be a large number of stops above 1.1250.

In order to think about ways that this may affect our trades going forward, it's important to understand that a large pool of stops or other orders can attract the exchange rate and pull it higher, so that those stops and orders will be executed. Why does this happen?

Remember that banks have a large role in the forex market, as the majority of forex volume passes through the Interbank, a loose affiliation of the world's largest banks. The customers of these banks place a variety of orders, and in many cases these banks earn a commission if and when these orders are executed.

Because of this, a large group of orders located together in one area becomes an attractive target. If the banks can manage to maneuver the

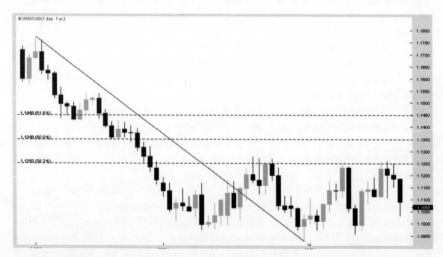

FIGURE 8.25 USD/CAD sellers step in repeatedly in the area of 1.1250.

Source: FXtrek IntelliChart™. Copyright © 2001–2006 FXtrek.com, Inc.

exchange rate so that these orders are executed, they will earn commissions. In this case, the likelihood of a large pool of stop orders above 1.1250 gives the banks an incentive to try to push USD/CAD higher.

This is easier said than done. The forex market is huge, and therefore it would be very expensive to attempt to manipulate the exchange rate in an overt manner. Banks cannot control exchange rates in the same manner that a specialist can control a listed stock on the New York Stock Exchange.

However, if the exchange rate is close to the "target" (that large pool of stops and other orders), one or more banks or other institutions might be tempted to give the exchange rate a little "push" to execute some of these orders.

By applying enough buying pressure at the right time, it might be possible for a bank to cause the exchange rate to reach the area above resistance where stops are located. This is more likely to happen during quiet times when liquidity is low.

This can create a chain reaction. Imagine that there are stops located just above 1.1250, and the banks are able to push the price up to a point where stops begin to execute. Since we already know that there has been considerable selling at 1.1250, then those stops exist to "cover," or close out, short positions.

Essentially, those stops are buy orders, because the only way to cover a short position is through buying. Imagine that stops are being hit at 1.1260; in this case, this really means that buy orders are being executed at 1.1260. This buying pressure at 1.1260 can push the exchange rate higher to 1.1270, where more stops are located. The chain reaction continues until many of the stops are eliminated.

As the price climbs above 1.1250, which had been such a great level of resistance, breakout traders will be tempted to enter long positions. Of course, you and I will not be tempted to do so, because this breakout is not in the direction of the primary trend.

All forms of trading, including forex, are susceptible to false breakouts, and breakouts that run in the opposite direction of the trend have a greater likelihood of failure. Still, not every trader takes this into consideration, and you can bet that some traders will be going long as the exchange rate rises above 1.1250.

As fate would have it, the USD/CAD pair did manage to break right through the Fibonacci resistance at 1.1250 (see Figure 8.26).

At this point, one of two things will happen—the breakout will either succeed or fail. If the breakout succeeds, that is fine with us, because we haven't sold short—at least not yet. We're not losing any money on the trade, and as a rule we don't worry about trades that we haven't entered.

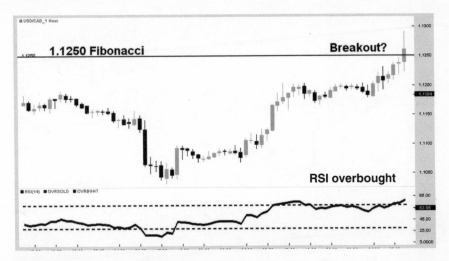

FIGURE 8.26 A possible breakout occurs in the opposite direction of the primary trend.

Source: FXtrek IntelliChart™. Copyright © 2001–2006 FXtrek.com, Inc.

If the exchange rate rises, it's going to have to do so without our participation.

But what if the breakout fails? I would consider the breakout to have failed if the exchange rate falls back beneath the breakout point of 1.1250. When this happens, it creates a compelling situation, as evidenced in Figure 8.27.

Remember the breakout traders who went long as the exchange rate climbed above 1.1250? How are they feeling now that the price has fallen below their entry point? They are feeling regret and discomfort, and are considering exiting the trade. Perhaps their stops are being triggered as the exchange rate falls.

As this group of traders closes out their losing positions, they are providing the fuel necessary to move the exchange rate lower. In other words, since they entered long positions above 1.1250 on the now-failed breakout, they must sell in order to cover their losing trades and exit the market.

This selling pressure helps to push the exchange rate lower, and also helps to create another entry point for traders wishing to sell the USD/CAD currency pair short. The short trader has all of the advantages of trading with the trend, with the added benefit of "help" from the breakout enthusiasts and trend fighters as they close their losing positions.

Also, remember that pool of stop orders and long entry orders that used to be located above 1.1250? Those orders acted like a magnet, pulling

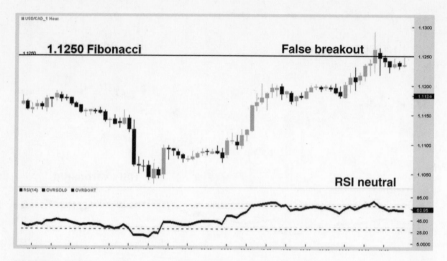

FIGURE 8.27 The breakout fails as the trend resumes; RSI falls from overbought levels.

Source: FXtrek IntelliChart™. Copyright © 2001–2006 FXtrek.com, Inc.

USD/CAD higher as banks sought to execute the orders and earn commissions.

It's interesting to note that after quickly rocketing toward 1.1300, the exchange rate fell back beneath 1.1250 within two hours. Once the orders were executed, there was no reason for the exchange rate to remain above 1.1250. The banks had earned their commissions, and as a result they no longer had any interest in supporting the pair.

Now there is no longer any reason for the banks and institutions to attempt to drive the exchange rate higher. As the breakout fails, the downtrend resumes and traders are presented with a new opportunity to short the USD/CAD pair (see Figure 8.28).

After a few candles pass, the exchange rate falls below 1.1190, triggering the first exit (see Figure 8.29). As per the previous plan, the trader exits the first lot of the trade. This also allows the trader to lower his stop to the breakeven entry point of 1.1225. The trader is thus assured of a small profit at the very least, while at the same time allowing the possibility of a larger gain.

This time, the pair bounces back and reaches our stop after we take our initial profit. Since the stop was lowered to 1.2225, we ended with a profit of 35 pips on the first lot and a break-even trade on lots two and three.

Over the next several days, more shorting opportunities presented themselves in the USD/CAD pair. Without reviewing each one individually,

FIGURE 8.28 Patience is rewarded as the USD/CAD short trade sets up once again.

Source: FXtrek IntelliChart™. Copyright © 2001–2006 FXtrek.com, Inc.

FIGURE 8.29 First exit is taken at 1.1190, and the stop is lowered to 1.1225.

Source: FXtrek IntelliChart™. Copyright © 2001–2006 FXtrek.com, Inc.

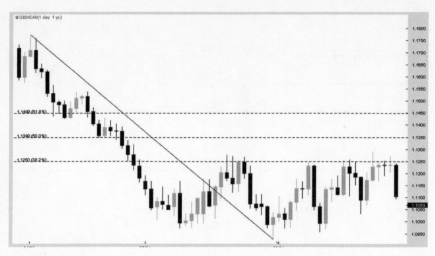

FIGURE 8.30 Many entry opportunities occurred at the Fibonacci level of 1.1250.

Source: FXtrek IntelliChart™. Copyright © 2001–2006 FXtrek.com, Inc.

we can say that overall, the trades worked out favorably, with only one setup resulting in a loss (35 pips on all three lots).

Several trades were mildly successful, and one trade was highly successful. This is significant not because of the number of winning trades versus losing trades, but because the size of the winning trades versus the size of the losing trade.

Figure 8.30 shows the Fibonacci on the daily chart, which was used as resistance for the original trade. Note that we have entered a series of mostly successful trades, even though the USD/CAD exchange rate really hasn't changed all that much on the daily chart.

A closer look reveals that reversal candles formed right at the Fibonacci resistance level, just prior to the exchange rate's latest plunge from the area of 1.1250. The two consecutive doji candles indicate that the bulls and bears had reached equilibrium, and points to the bulls' earlier failure to hold the exchange rate above 1.1250 (see Figure 8.31).

By following along with this series of trades, we've seen exactly the type of strategies that trend following traders can use to trade profitably. More than just a specific technique, we have also examined the philosophy behind this style of trading, and the various thought processes that sometimes derail an otherwise successful trade of this nature.

I hope that I've provided a warts-and-all example showing that things sometimes do not go exactly according to plan, because in the real world, they simply don't. I realize that there are people trying to sell you on the

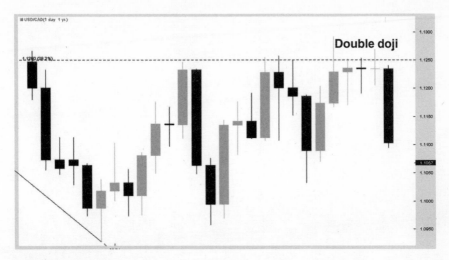

FIGURE 8.31 Doji reversal candles confirm Fibonacci resistance.

Source: FXtrek IntelliChart™. Copyright © 2001–2006 FXtrek.com, Inc.

idea that you can "win" all the time, but in reality, the market does not always cooperate.

That's why the built-in risk management plan is so important; the method for moving the stop is designed to prevent damage to your account when the market does not cooperate. It also allows the trader to realize substantial gains under more favorable trading conditions.

While not everything went according to plan, we learned not to worry about things we cannot control, such as what happens after we enter a trade. Instead, we focus our attention on those things that we can control, such as creating a good trading plan and executing it to the best of our ability. If we can do that on a consistent basis, our chances for long-term trading success will increase dramatically.

CHAPTER 9

The FX-Ed Trend Technique

Earlier, we compared a trend to a river, and we noted that it is easier to paddle in the direction of the current than it is to fight our way upstream. Each river has its own current, and the strength of that current can, and sometimes does, change. Sometimes a drought will dry the flow to a trickle, bringing the river to a near standstill. At other times, great storms will cause floods and turn the river into an unstoppable force.

How should we approach a trending market situation when the usual "current" becomes a roaring, foaming whitewater rapid? We've already looked at techniques for trading with the trend, but there are times when trends can become overwhelmingly strong and require a more aggressive approach. Why do some trends become so strong?

TRENDS ARE SELF-SUSTAINING

One reason this happens is that the longer a market trends, the more obvious that trend becomes. The longer duration makes it easier for other participants to identify the trend and join in. As more and more traders climb aboard in the same direction, the trend accelerates and takes on a life of its own.

The action becomes self-sustaining, as traders who are seeking to take advantage of the trend are in effect forcing the trend to continue. This is one of the reasons why trends tend to continue for longer periods of time than most traders anticipate, and why we should never try to pick the top or bottom of a trend.

DIFFERENCE OF OPINION

Another reason to consider is that since each currency pair contains two currencies, we are sometimes faced with an imbalance in the perception of the economies of those two countries. Perhaps one economy is perceived as strong, and traders perceive that it will become even stronger. This strength, or perceived strength, will be reflected in the currency of that country. As a result, the currency of that country rallies.

At the same time, the opposite may be true for the opposing currency; traders may believe that the economy is weak and perhaps it will grow weaker. This perceived weakness would be reflected in the currency of that country, and as a result the latter currency would suffer in comparison to the former currency.

If there is a vastly different perception in the strength and/or weakness of the two currencies in the pair, the exchange rate must move to reflect this disparity. Sometimes, the exchange rate must rise or fall a great distance before these perceptions are fully reflected.

BIG MONEY AT WORK

If a trend is very strong and persistent, it's likely that the "big money" of institutional traders is at work. Let's face it; the forex market is so huge that a strong trend cannot be sustained for long without the tremendous amounts of capital these big players pour into the market. This is very different from the equity market, where a few individuals placing large orders can drive the price activity of an illiquid stock.

THE COMMON DENOMINATOR

If we observe past situations where currency pairs have launched into strong trends, we can find some common denominators. One of these is the tendency for the exchange rate to pull back to a key moving average before resuming the trend.

In particular, there is considerable evidence that in extremely strong trends, pullbacks (in the case of an uptrend) or rallies (in the case of a

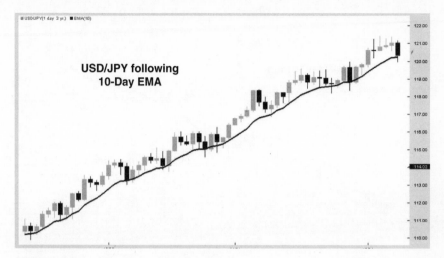

FIGURE 9.1   USD/JPY climbing the 10-Day Exponential Moving Average.

Source: FXtrek IntelliChart™. Copyright © 2001–2006 FXtrek.com, Inc.

downtrend) to the 10-day exponential moving average make particularly effective entry points for forex traders. This is because the big players are using this moving average to determine their entry points as well.

For example, here we see the U.S. dollar/Japanese yen (USD/JPY) currency pair trending higher in the second half of 2005 (see Figure 9.1). Notice how tightly the exchange rate hugs the 10-day exponential moving average (EMA). The pair gained more than 1,200 pips in less than four months, and bounced repeatedly off of the 10-day EMA.

Traders who use Ichimoku indicators may notice that in this case, the price activity in USD/JPY was also very closely aligned with the Tenkan line, an indicator that is widely used in Japan, and by yen traders everywhere (see Figure 9.2). When trading one of the yen currency pairs, this could be used as confirmation for the 10-day EMA, but for our purposes, we will focus on the 10-day exponential moving average only.

Figure 9.3 shows another example, with the euro/U.S. dollar (EUR/USD) currency pair scaling the 10-day EMA during the second half of 2003.

LONG OR SHORT

We see this occur in currency pairs that are falling as well as rising. In Figure 9.4, the U.S. dollar is falling versus the Canadian dollar in the fall of 2003. In fact, during that time, the U.S. dollar was losing ground against

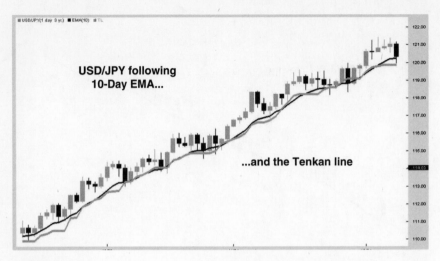

FIGURE 9.2 In this case, the Tenkan Line provided additional support for USD/JPY.

Source: FXtrek IntelliChart™. Copyright © 2001–2006 FXtrek.com, Inc.

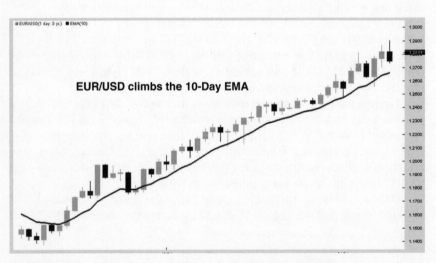

FIGURE 9.3 The EUR/USD currency pair scales the 10-day EMA.

Source: FXtrek IntelliChart™. Copyright © 2001–2006 FXtrek.com, Inc.

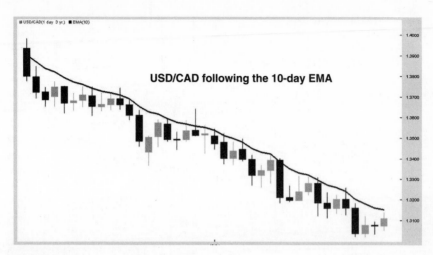

FIGURE 9.4 10-day EMA acting as resistance on the USD/CAD currency pair.

Source: FXtrek IntelliChart™. Copyright © 2001–2006 FXtrek.com, Inc.

most of the major currencies, and on many of the charts at that time the 10-day EMA was clearly coming into play. Why does this keep happening?

Institutional traders are buying on the dips in the case of an uptrend, or selling the rallies during a downtrend. The 10-day moving average is a convenient location for these big players to either open new positions or add to existing positions during a runaway trend. They are entering the trade in the direction of the trend, but by waiting for the exchange rate to return to the moving average, they avoid entering at an extreme level.

IDENTIFYING THE TREND

The exchange rate is showing a tendency to bounce off of this moving average during a strong trend. How can we benefit from this market tendency?

The first thing that we need to do is determine whether or not the market is actually trending. One of the worst things that we can do is to just randomly use a trend-following technique when the market is not trending. Let's look at several different options to determine if a currency pair is setting up properly for this technique.

The first option will be what traders refer to as the "proper order" of moving averages. For our purposes, we can define the proper order of moving averages in an uptrend as:

1. The 10-day moving average is above the 20-day moving average.
2. The 20-day moving average is above the 50-day moving average.
3. The 50-day moving average is above the 200-day moving average.

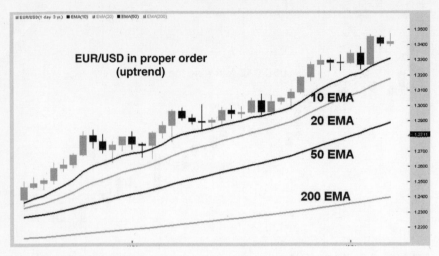

FIGURE 9.5 EUR/USD moving averages are in the "proper order" for an uptrend. *Source*: FXtrek IntelliChart™. Copyright © 2001–2006 FXtrek.com, Inc.

Figure 9.5 shows the EUR/USD currency pair, breaking into an uptrend as the moving averages assemble themselves in the proper order.

In the event of a downtrend, the proper order of moving averages would be defined as:

1. The 200-day moving average is above the 50-day moving average.
2. The 50-day moving average is above the 20-day moving average.
3. The 20-day moving average is above the 10-day moving average.

Figure 9.6 shows the U.S. dollar/Swiss franc (USD/CHF) currency pair, trending lower as the moving averages align themselves in the proper order for a downtrend. Note that this occurs during the same period of time that the EUR/USD is trending higher on the previous chart (Figure 9.5). Since these two currency pairs have a high negative correlation, it's not unusual to see this type of simultaneous trending behavior.

FILTERING THE TREND

Using this method to determine the trend can be very effective, but at the same time it can also be limiting. Remember, we are focused on the 10-day

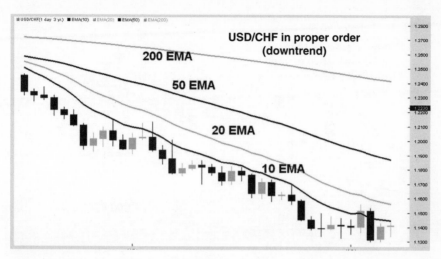

FIGURE 9.6 USD/CHF moving averages are in the "proper order" for a downtrend.

Source: FXtrek IntelliChart™. Copyright © 2001–2006 FXtrek.com, Inc.

EMA, so we need to add a filter based on this moving average. Because this technique is designed to benefit from a strong trend, we need to be certain that this is not an ordinary trend.

Let's add this caveat: In addition to having the moving averages aligned in the proper order, if we can clearly see evidence that the 10-day moving average is acting as either support (in the case of an uptrend) or resistance (in the case of a downtrend) on the daily chart for a period of at least 10 days, then we can enter a trade based on this technique. Just be certain that you are seeing real evidence, and not using some form of wishful thinking to enter a trade. How can we be sure?

Here's our filter: Not only must we have our moving averages lined up correctly, but the exchange rate must be above the 10-day exponential moving average for a period of at least 10 or more candles in the case of an uptrend. In the case of a downtrend, we need to see the exchange rate trapped below the 10-day EMA for a period of at least 10 or more candles.

Figure 9.7 is an example of how to use this filter; in the example below, the Great Britain pound/Japanese yen currency pair (GBP/JPY) has aligned its moving averages in the proper order, yet there is no evidence of support at the 10-day EMA.

The exchange rate cuts above and below the 10-day EMA repeatedly and in both directions, as if it were not there. Why would we want to base a trade on the 10-day moving average when we can plainly see that it is not acting as support?

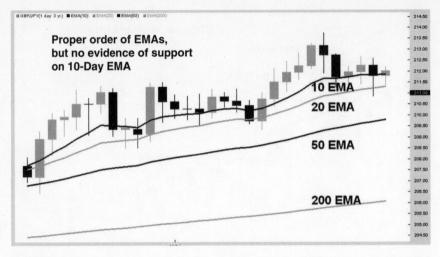

FIGURE 9.7 In this case, although the moving averages are in proper order, there is no evidence of support at the 10-Day EMA.

Source: FXtrek IntelliChart™. Copyright © 2001–2006 FXtrek.com, Inc.

If this were truly a strong trend, the institutional buyers would not wait for the exchange rate to drop below the moving average; they would be adding to positions as the price falls, causing the exchange rate to bounce back up when it reaches the 10-day EMA.

By adding this filter, we can avoid entering trades if the big players are not sufficiently committed to adding to their positions. If the major players are hesitant about increasing the size of their positions, they may not be the "strong hands" that are necessary to keep this trend moving higher.

Now, let's take a look at an example where the 10-day EMA clearly is acting as support. On the daily chart of the EUR/USD currency pair, we can see that not only are the moving averages aligned in their proper order, but also that the exchange rate is consistently above the 10-day EMA (see Figure 9.8).

Occasionally, we see the exchange rate dip below the 10-day EMA, but these excursions are only temporary, as the price quickly bounces back. This happens because the institutional traders are committed to their positions, and are willing to add to them as the exchange rate dips to the moving average.

This is exactly the type of situation that we are hoping for; we have a strong trend that is supported by institutional buying. The big players are enthusiastic enough about this trend that they are willing to add to their positions in an aggressive manner.

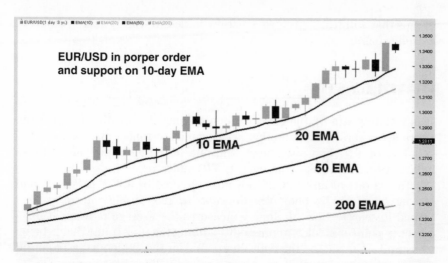

FIGURE 9.8 In addition to the proper order of moving averages, we see evidence of support at the 10-day EMA.

Source: FXtrek IntelliChart™. Copyright © 2001–2006 FXtrek.com, Inc.

THE CATALYST

Often, the catalyst for this aggressive buying is a widening interest rate differential; in other words, one of the currencies involved in the trade has a rising interest rate, and the other currency has a steady or falling interest rate. This situation frequently occurs during the interest rate arbitrage trade, also known as the *carry trade*.

If a strong trend exists, and the exchange rate is finding support at the 10-day EMA, then we will enter our trade as the exchange rate reaches the 10-day EMA. The first consideration will be where to place the protective stop; indeed, we will not even enter the trade unless we have already determined a suitable location for the stop.

PLACING THE STOP

In this trade, we have already determined that the 10-day EMA is the entry point and the basis for our trade. Therefore, if we are long, our stop must be located underneath the 10-day EMA. But how far away should the stop be placed? Are there a certain number of pips that we should use, or should we look to other levels and forms of support?

Since major support is already incorporated into the trade in the form of the 10-day EMA, we need another solution. There is no "magic number" of pips that will work, because volatility varies so widely among different currency pairs.

VOLATILITY STOP

This volatility will be the basis for determining the location of our stop. There are several indicators that are designed to reflect and measure the volatility of a trading instrument, and one of the most popular of these indicators is the average true range (ATR) indicator.

This is one of an array of indicators created by J.Welles Wilder, and was introduced in his book *New Concepts in Technical Trading Systems* (Trend Research, 1978). It simply measures the average movement for a currency pair (or stock, or commodity) during the time frame that is being measured (in this case, the daily chart). Wilder recommended a 14-period default for measuring ATR, so that is what we will use for this strategy.

For example, the GBP/USD currency pair shows an ATR (14 periods) of 0.0148, which would translate to an average daily range of 148 pips. This means that for the past 14 days, the pair has moved, on average, 148 pips per day. We can see that the average daily range was previously as high as 190 pips per day (see Figure 9.9).

Compare the average range for GBP/USD to the average daily range for the EUR/GBP currency pair; the latter pair shows an ATR of only 0.0035, or just 35 pips per day (see Figure 9.10).

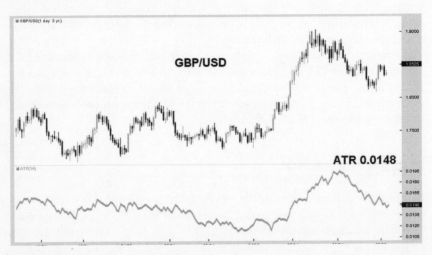

FIGURE 9.9 The average true range (ATR) measures the volatility of a currency pair. Here, the GBP/USD daily chart shows an ATR of 148 pips.

Source: FXtrek IntelliChart™. Copyright © 2001–2006 FXtrek.com, Inc.

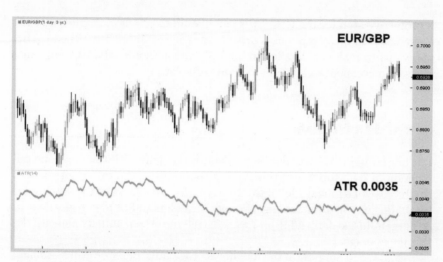

FIGURE 9.10 Volatility can vary widely from one currency pair to another. Here, the daily chart of the EUR/GBP pair shows an ATR of just 35 pips.

Source: FXtrek IntelliChart™. Copyright © 2001–2006 FXtrek.com, Inc.

Let's think about this for a minute: One currency pair moves about 148 pips per day, and the other moves about 35 pips per day. Imagine that a protective stop is placed at an appropriate distance (i.e., "x" number of pips) for one pair. Would a stop placed at this distance also be appropriate for the other, if the two pairs are in similar situations?

COMPARING APPLES TO APPLES

The answer is: most definitely not. Consider a 30-pip stop; this might be considered a close stop for the GBP/USD currency pair, because 30 pips is equal to just about 20 percent of the average daily range of that pair (148 pips). Meanwhile, a 30-pip stop could be considered a wide stop for the EUR/GBP pair, because it is equal to nearly 90 percent of the pair's average daily range of 35 pips.

Because of this, a 30-pip stop (or any fixed number of pips) cannot be considered an effective stop in every situation, because volatility varies so widely from one currency pair to another. While we can't use a fixed number of pips in an effective manner, we can use the ATR indicator to help calculate the location of our stop.

Consider the difference in ATR readings in the above example; GBP/USD's average daily range is more than four times the average daily range of EUR/GBP. So it stands to reason that, all other things being equal, a protective stop for the GBP/USD pair should be about four times as wide (four times as many pips) as a protective stop for the EUR/GBP pair. This allows us to make an "apples to apples" comparison of the two currency pairs, and compensates for the variable of volatility.

ATR CALCULATION

For our strategy, we will use 50 percent of the daily ATR to determine the location of our stop. Since this strategy is based on the theory of support (in the case of a long trade) at the 10-day EMA, we will place the stop under the 10-day exponential moving average by an amount of pips equivalent to 50 percent of the daily ATR, and we will trail the stop manually beneath the moving average.

This way, if support at the moving average fails, our stop will be hit and we will be taken out of the trade. However, as long as the moving average support holds, we can remain in the trade, and then trail the stop higher if the trend remains intact.

Huge Potential

If we are fortunate and the pair continues trending strongly, the potential exists for a big winning trade. When we enter a trade of this nature, the best-case scenario would be that the pair continues to trend for a very long time. When this happens, the size of a winning trade can become astounding.

In this example, we see the EUR/USD currency pair is in an uptrend. The moving averages are in the proper order for an uptrend, and the exchange rate has remained above the 10-day EMA for at least 10 days (see Figure 9.11). We have met the necessary criteria to enter the trade.

THE ENTRY

As the exchange rate falls to the 10-day EMA, we'll enter a long position. We can enter as soon as we observe the exchange rate dipping to the moving average; there is no need to wait for the candle to close. The entry point is 1.2645

Now that we have entered the trade, we need to calculate the location of the stop. The trader measures the ATR (14 periods) for the daily chart, and the result is 0.0110 (see Figure 9.12). This is another way of saying that the average daily range of EUR/USD is 110 pips per day at this time.

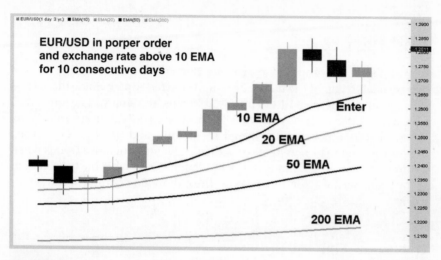

FIGURE 9.11 The EUR/USD pair meets the proper criteria to enter a trade.

Source: FXtrek IntelliChart™. Copyright © 2001–2006 FXtrek.com, Inc.

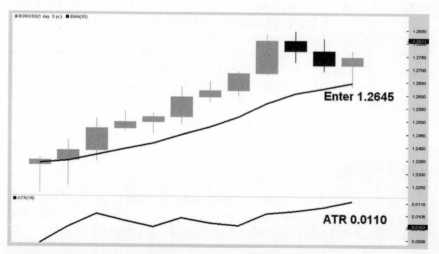

FIGURE 9.12 The trade is entered as the exchange rate falls to the 10-day EMA. The ATR measures 110 pips, so the stop will be placed 55 pips beneath the EMA.

Source: FXtrek IntelliChart™. Copyright © 2001–2006 FXtrek.com, Inc.

THE STOP

We will locate the stop underneath the 10-day EMA, by a number of pips that is equal to half of the daily range of the currency pair. Since the ATR is 110 pips, and 50 percent of 110 pips is = 55 pips, the stop will be located 55 pips beneath our entry point of 1.2645. This places our initial stop at 1.2590.

Since this strategy is designed to identify and exploit very strong trends, we want to be sure that we take full advantage of those trends when we do find them. The point is that we shouldn't be in a big hurry to get out of the trade because, for all we know, the pair might continue trending for weeks.

Trailing the Stop

Let's acknowledge this point by designing the stop so that we can trail it along beneath the moving average, instead of aiming for a specific target. We will raise the stop every time a daily candle closes.

Since we are trading within an uptrend, we will not lower the stop under any circumstances. We will keep the stop beneath the 10-day EMA, at an amount equal to 50 percent of the daily ATR, until the exchange rate finally breaks down and reaches our stop.

The initial entry and stop are calculated according to the current (open) daily candle, but as the trade progresses we will move the stop and calculate the ATR and the 10-day EMA according to the most recently closed candle.

THE TRADE

On Day 1, we enter the trade at 1.2645. After we enter, the exchange rate continues to dip to about 1.2630 (see Figure 9.13). Because our initial stop at 1.2590 was not reached, the trade continues into the next day.

On Day 2, our stop is not hit as the exchange rate is now firmly above the 10-day EMA (see Figure 9.14).

We do not raise the stop, because from this point on the protective stop must be calculated according to the most recently closed candle. Since the most recently closed candle is the same candle that was open when we entered the trade, we cannot raise our stop yet. The daily ATR dips to 0.0109.

Finally, the Day 2 candle closes, and we enter Day 3, and we can now raise the stop. First, we must calculate the 10-day EMA for the most

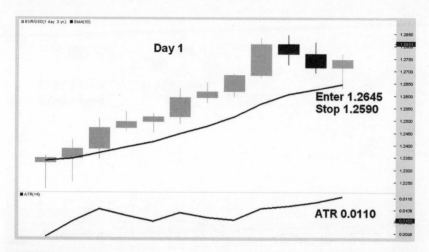

FIGURE 9.13 The exchange rate dips briefly beneath the moving average on the first day of the trade. This is when the risk is greatest.

Source: FXtrek IntelliChart™. Copyright © 2001–2006 FXtrek.com, Inc.

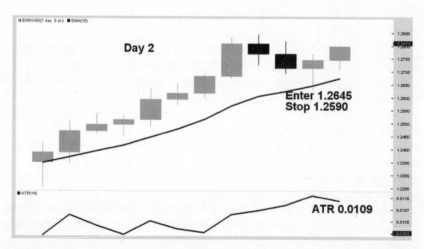

FIGURE 9.14 The stop cannot be raised until the Day 2 daily candle is closed.

Source: FXtrek IntelliChart™. Copyright © 2001–2006 FXtrek.com, Inc.

recently closed (Day 2) candle. We can see that the 10-day EMA has now climbed to 1.2673 (see Figure 9.15).

The ATR is still perched at 110 pips, so the stop must be raised so that it is 55 pips (half of the ATR) beneath the moving average. This means that as Day 3 begins, we can raise our stop to 1.2618 (the new location of the exponential moving average of 1.2673 minus 55 pips).

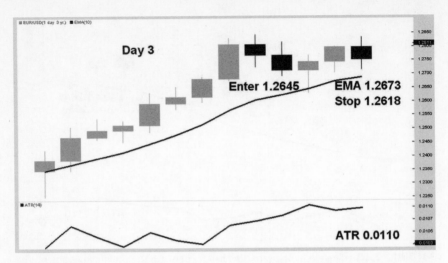

FIGURE 9.15 On Day 3, the stop is raised to keep pace with the moving average.

Source: FXtrek IntelliChart™. Copyright © 2001–2006 FXtrek.com, Inc.

Note that our risk was originally 55 pips per lot, and now this has been reduced to 27 pips per lot (entry of 1.2645 minus the new stop of 1.2618). If we can continue raising the stop, we will further reduce, and perhaps eliminate, any remaining risk from the trade.

As the candle closes on Day 3, the moving average has risen to 1.2687, and the ATR has dropped to 108 (see Figure 9.16). Our stop will be placed beneath the moving average by 54 pips (50 percent of the ATR reading of 108), so our stop will be raised to 1.2633 (1.2687 minus 54 pips). Since our entry point was 1.2645, we have now lowered the risk on this trade to 12 pips per lot (1.2645 entry, 1.2633 stop).

During the Day 4 candle, the exchange rate dips beneath the 10-day EMA for the first time since our entry. However, the low of the Day 4 candle is 1.2664, so our stop of 1.2633 is untouched and the trade continues. As long as the exchange rate doesn't fall sharply below the 10-day EMA, the trade is still alive.

As the Day 4 candle closes, and we enter Day 5, the 10-day EMA has moved up again, this time to 1.2698 (see Figure 9.17). The ATR reading is still 108, and half of 108 = 54, so our stop is trailed higher to 1.2644 (1.2698 minus 54 pips = 1.2644). Our total risk on this trade has now been reduced to one pip per lot.

During Day 5, we get quite a scare as the exchange rate dives beneath the 10-day EMA again, falling to 1.2656, missing our stop by just 12 pips

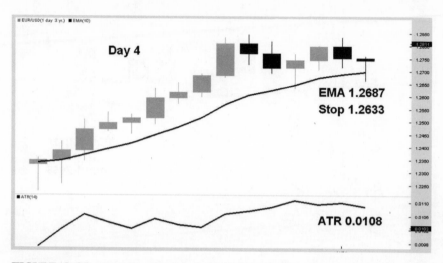

FIGURE 9.16 Now that the Day 3 candle has closed, the stop is raised again, and is now placed 54 pips beneath the EMA to compensate for the slight reduction in ATR.

Source: FXtrek IntelliChart™. Copyright © 2001–2006 FXtrek.com, Inc.

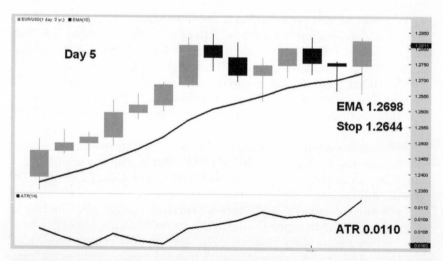

FIGURE 9.17 The Day 4 candle closes, and we enter Day 5. A close call as the exchange rate falls through the EMA and nearly reaches the stop.

Source: FXtrek IntelliChart™. Copyright © 2001–2006 FXtrek.com, Inc.

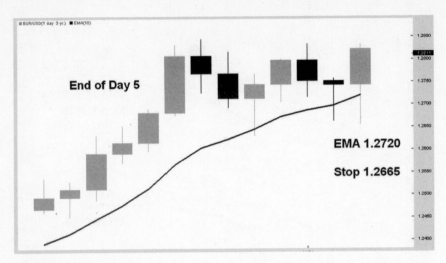

FIGURE 9.18 After the Day 5 candle closes, we raise the stop again. The stop is now above the entry point.

Source: FXtrek IntelliChart™. Copyright © 2001–2006 FXtrek.com, Inc.

before reversing and bouncing back above the moving average. Luckily, institutional traders use the dip to add to their positions, and by the time the Day 5 candle closes, the exchange rate is back above 1.2800, and the moving average has climbed to 1.2720 (see Figure 9.18).

The added volatility has caused the ATR to bounce back up to 110, so the next time we calculate our stop, it will be located 55 pips (50 percent of 110) beneath the 10-day EMA. This raises our protective stop to 1.2665 (1.2720 minus 55 pips = 1.2665).

Not only has all of the risk been eliminated from the trade, our stop is now 20 pips above our entry point of 1.2645. Our worst-case scenario is a gain of 20 pips per lot, but if the pair continues to trend, our profit could be considerably larger.

Let's jump ahead to Day 17; since we survived our close call on Day 5, the exchange rate has slipped beneath the 10-day EMA once, and just by a few pips (see Figure 9.19). Therefore, our stop has not been threatened, as the EUR/USD currency pair continues to trend higher.

By the end of Day 17, the moving average has climbed all the way to 1.2947, and our stop has been trailed higher to 1.2892. Since we entered this trade 17 days earlier at 1.2645, our stop is now 247 pips above our entry point. Our worst-case scenario is now a gain of 247 pips per lot! Remember, our risk on the trade was never more than 55 pips per lot.

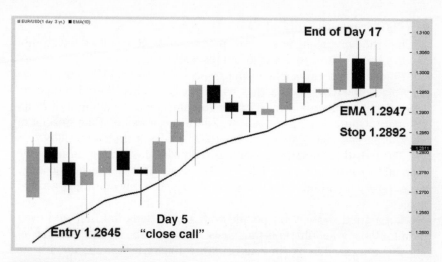

FIGURE 9.19 Days 5 through 17: since the exchange rate has barely touched the EMA, the stop has not been hit and the trade is still in effect.

Source: FXtrek IntelliChart™. Copyright © 2001–2006 FXtrek.com, Inc.

DON'T FISH FOR MINNOWS

At this point, I'm sure some of you are thinking, "Ed, I only want to gain 10 pips per day; I don't want to hold my trades for 17 days!" Try to look at it this way: If you had actually gained 10 pips per day, for 17 consecutive days, you would have gained only 170 pips profit versus our worst-case scenario of 247 pips. Plus, if this trend continues, the gain may become even larger.

Also, if you are placing short-term trades with a small profit potential, you are paying the spread over and over again. The spread is your number one obstacle to profitability, and the more often you pay it, the more of your money you are giving away to the market maker. An active, short-term trader is the market maker's best friend. Not to mention the fact that you are working very hard. Short-term trading is very labor intensive!

Meanwhile, the trader using the FX-Ed Trend Technique is moving the stop once per day. That's it. As they say in the business world, "Do you want to work harder, or do you want to work smarter?"

Plus, I think you'll find that once you place a trade that earns hundreds of pips, you might find it difficult to go back to your old ways. You'll wonder why you've been wasting your time picking up pennies off the ground when

Low-Maintenance Method

This method of trading is very low maintenance. Remember, we are not involved in a contest to see who can place the most trades.

Some traders, especially novices, seem to think that the more trades they place, the more money they will make. In reality, there is no correlation between the number of trades you place and the amount of profit you earn. One really good trade will earn more money than dozens of mediocre trades, so I encourage you to choose your trades carefully.

The only thing that the trader has to do with this strategy is move the stop once per day, after the daily candle closes. This is a perfect strategy for people who do not want to spend their entire day staring at a video screen.

It's a great strategy for people who are working full time and can't monitor the market on a constant basis. Or it could be a longer-term strategy that a trader can use in conjunction with shorter-term strategies. As we will see from the various strategies discussed in this book, there is no need to limit ourselves to just one strategy!

all the while there was real money to be made. Why fish for minnows when there are bigger fish in the sea?

BACK TO THE TRADE

Let's jump ahead again, this time to Day 27 (see Figure 9.20). Just by glancing at the chart, we know that the stop has not been hit because it is well under the 10-day EMA, which has been touched only sporadically since our "close call" on Day 5. There have been no incursions of more than a few pips since then, and clearly, big traders are "loading the boat" every time the exchange rate drops to the moving average.

The 10-day EMA is now all the way up to 1.3256, and the ATR, bolstered by the increase in volatility, has risen to 118 pips per day (not shown). 118 divided by 2 = 59, so the stop must now be placed 59 pips beneath the moving average, at 1.3197 (1.3256 minus 59 pips = 1.3197).

This means that we have now locked in a profit of 552 pips (the stop of 1.3197, minus the entry point of 1.2645 = 552 pips). Even if our stop is hit tomorrow, we are holding a substantial gain!

All good things must come to an end, and this trade is no different. Two days later, on Day 29, the moving average has climbed to 1.3308 (see Figure 9.21). The ATR has backed off a bit to 112, so our stop will be placed 56 pips (50 percent of 112) beneath the moving average, at 1.3252.

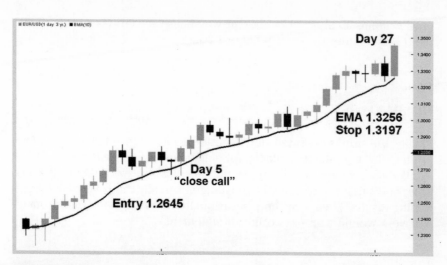

FIGURE 9.20 The exchange rate remains above the EMA through Day 27. Because the ATR has climbed to 118 pips per day, the stop is 59 pips beneath the EMA.

Source: FXtrek IntelliChart™. Copyright © 2001–2006 FXtrek.com, Inc.

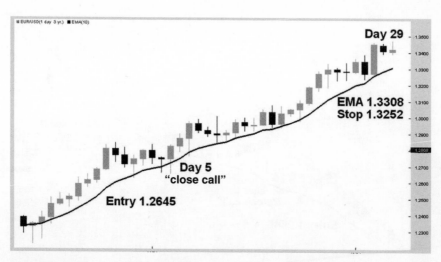

FIGURE 9.21 The moving average continues to rise, and on Day 29 we raise the stop for what will be the final time.

Source: FXtrek IntelliChart™. Copyright © 2001–2006 FXtrek.com, Inc.

(1.3308 minus 56 pips = 1.3252). Our worst-case scenario is a profit of 607 pips (1.3252 minus the entry point of 1.2645).

DENOUEMENT

Finally, the stop is executed, and the trade is closed (see Figure 9.22). Our profit of 607 pips should make up for quite a few small losses!

We can't expect the FX-Ed Trend Technique to work this well every time, but it takes only a few large winners to really improve your overall trading results. Even if we only occasionally capture an outsized profit, it will work wonders for our profit/loss statement.

THE NEWS VERSUS THE TREND

What happens when political or economic events clash with a strong trend? If the trend meets all of the criteria as mentioned earlier, then any type of news event that creates a reaction against the trend is likely to have only a temporary effect. For an example of this, I'd like to take you back to the year 2003.

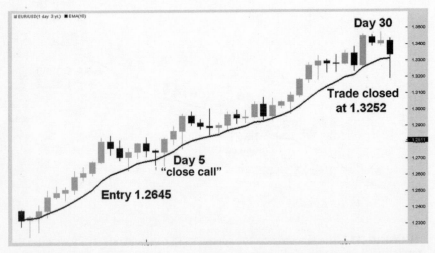

FIGURE 9.22 The exchange rate collapses and falls sharply beneath the 10-Day EMA, and the stop is finally executed at 1.3252.

Source: FXtrek IntelliChart™. Copyright © 2001–2006 FXtrek.com, Inc.

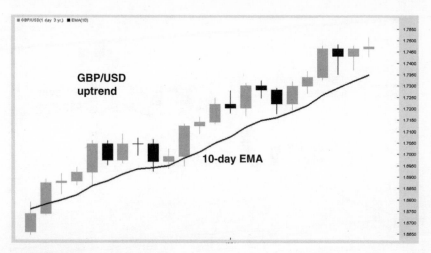

FIGURE 9.23 A strong uptrend in GBP/USD in late 2003. Moving averages are in the proper order for an uptrend (not shown).

Source: FXtrek IntelliChart™. Copyright © 2001–2006 FXtrek.com, Inc.

At that time, the United States had invaded Iraq, and Saddam Hussein, the deposed leader of the Iraq, had gone into hiding. During the second half of the year, the U.S. dollar was in a steep downtrend against most of the major currencies of the world, including the Great Britain pound.

Here we can see about a month's worth of activity, with the GBP/USD pair finding support repeatedly at the 10-day EMA (see Figure 9.23). The 10, 20, 50 and 200 period EMAs are in the proper order for an uptrend (not shown).

During a mid-December weekend, the news spread that Hussein had been captured in Iraq. It was early on a Sunday in New York when I heard the news, so the markets weren't open yet. We had plenty of time to absorb all of the available information and consider the possible consequences of this event. To many traders, it seemed that this was good news for the U.S. dollar.

When trading commenced a few hours later, the knee-jerk reaction of the market was a stronger U.S. dollar, and the buck quickly gained across the board. Within a few minutes of the open, then GBP/USD pair fell 120 pips, reflecting the strength of the dollar bulls, who appeared to be in control—or so it seemed at the time.

APPEARANCES CAN BE DECEIVING

Trend traders had a different perspective on the situation. GBP/USD was clearly in a roaring uptrend, and the sudden USD strength created an entry

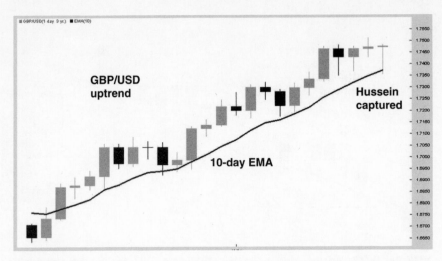

FIGURE 9.24 U.S. dollar bulls, excited by the capture of Saddam Hussein, push the exchange rate down to the 10-day EMA.

Source: FXtrek IntelliChart™. Copyright © 2001–2006 FXtrek.com, Inc.

opportunity for trend traders, as the currency pair dipped below its 10-day EMA.

Instead of climbing aboard the "buy the U.S. dollar" bandwagon, trend traders looked at the bigger picture and followed their plan. The dip had created an excellent entry point to go long the British pound against the U.S. dollar. By the time the daily candle closed, traders who entered long on the 10-day EMA had earned a profit of over 100 pips in just a few hours (see Figure 9.24).

I'm sure that many traders happily took the 100-pip profit and closed the trade, but those who stuck with the trade were rewarded handsomely. The trend, which had been so evident prior to Hussein's capture, was still very much alive. In fact, 23 trading days would pass before the price would again make contact with the 10-day EMA (see Figure 9.25).

The entry point for this trade, placed on December 15, 2003, was 1.7372. The next time the exchange rate made contact with the 10-day EMA, the moving average was located at 1.8233 (see Figure 9.26). The ATR reading was 160, so our stop would be placed 80 pips beneath the moving average, at 1.8153. That stop would be executed on Day 24, and the gain from the trade would equal 781 pips per lot (1.8153 exit, minus the entry point of 1.7372 = 781 pips).

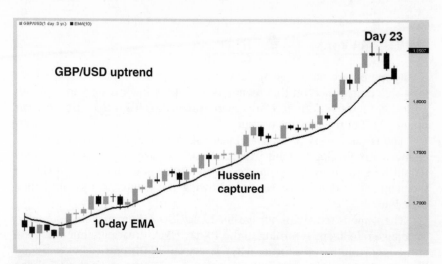

FIGURE 9.25 Nearly a month would pass before the GBP/USD exchange rate again touched the 10-day EMA.

Source: FXtrek IntelliChart™. Copyright © 2001–2006 FXtrek.com, Inc.

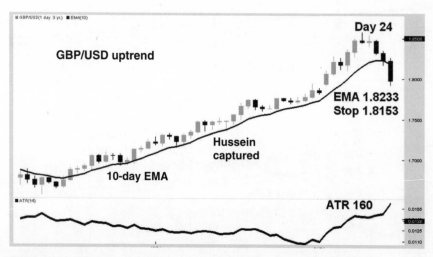

FIGURE 9.26 The stop is executed on Day 24, after a substantial gain.

Source: FXtrek IntelliChart™. Copyright © 2001–2006 FXtrek.com, Inc.

MORE THAN ONE CHANCE

Even long before the Hussein trade, there were numerous chances to go long this pair, based on this technique. Looking back over a four-month period in Figure 9.27, notice how many times the GBP/USD currency pair bounced off of the moving average.

Though not every trade would have been successful, there were many chances for profitable long trades. Also, the size of the losing trades would be limited by the protective stop. There is no limit to the size of the winning trades, since we are allowing the trends to run until they collapse.

The same is true with our earlier EUR/USD example. Notice how the exchange rate keeps returning to the 10-day EMA, creating numerous long entry opportunities (see Figure 9.28). Every one of the entries below would have resulted in a successful trade, with the exception of the Day 27 entry, which would have resulted in a small loss.

This abundance of opportunities teaches us that we should not "chase" after a missed entry, because there are often many available chances to enter a trade.

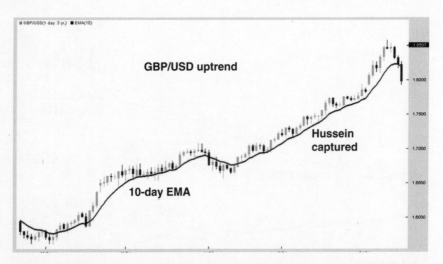

FIGURE 9.27 Prior to Hussein's capture, there were many entry opportunities based on this technique. While some of the entries failed, the majority led to successful trades.

Source: FXtrek IntelliChart™. Copyright © 2001–2006 FXtrek.com, Inc.

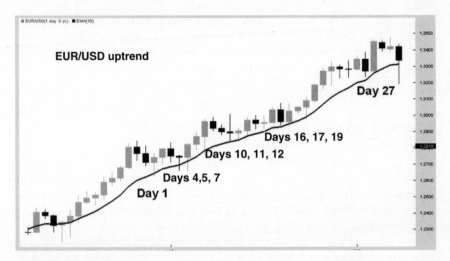

FIGURE 9.28 Numerous long entry opportunities for the EUR/USD pair.

Source: FXtrek IntelliChart™. Copyright © 2001–2006 FXtrek.com, Inc.

PARTIAL EXIT EXERCISE

You may have noticed that some strategies possess built-in techniques for exiting a trade in a piecemeal fashion. At this point, you may be wondering how to execute a partial exit from this type of trade.

This technique is based on a strong trend. It might end at any time, or it might continue for weeks or months. There is no way to know for certain what will happen next. A strong trend allows traders to be more aggressive with their exits, because the nature of a trend is that it keeps moving in one direction, away from the entry point.

In a range-bound market, we need to be more conservative with our targets, because the nature of a rangebound market is that the exchange rate eventually reverses direction and comes back toward the entry point.

In a strongly trending market, we want to give our winning trades more room to run, and we are trying to give this particular trend trade a chance to become a big winner. This means that we have to be more aggressive than usual with our targets. In fact, we are simply letting the trade run until the exchange rate collapses into the moving average. This is why we haven't discussed exits, other than the stop, up to this point.

However, there are techniques that we can apply to this strategy to create partial exits. Before we get into this partial exit technique, I want you to try an exercise that is *not* a part of this trading style that will teach you a valuable lesson about trading with the trend.

DISCRETIONARY AND STRATEGIC EXITS

When you are practicing this technique in a demo account (and I highly recommend that you practice *every* technique that you learn *repeatedly* in a demo account), try the following exercise: You can exit half of the trade at any point that you wish, as long as you exit the second half of the trade only in the manner described in the FX-Ed Trend Technique.

In other words, you can exit half of the position at any time, for any reason, as long as you follow the technique correctly with the second half of the trade, by trailing the stop underneath the 10-day EMA. We will refer to the first exit as a "discretionary exit" and the second exit as the "strategic exit."

I want you to do this exercise repeatedly in a demo account, and keep track of your results in a trading journal. After you have done this for a while, most of you will notice that the discretionary exit is rarely as good as the strategic exit. Why does this happen?

FAULTY WIRING

The reason is that, as human beings, we are wired to exit our trades too quickly. Think about the examples that we reviewed earlier; how many people do you think will hold on to a profitable trade long enough to gain hundreds of pips? The fact is that few of us have the discipline to hold on to winning trades for that length of time.

We need to have rules and strategies that will keep us in a strongly trending trade, even when we "feel" that we should get out. Left to our own devices, we will almost always exit our good trades too soon and hold on to our bad trades for too long.

Just in case anyone is not clear on this, I do *not* recommend exiting half of the position at your discretion once you are trading this style in a *live* account. This is an *exercise*, the purpose of which is to teach us this: *We will be better off if we simply follow the plan and disregard our own opinions or feelings about the trade.*

PARTIAL EXIT TECHNIQUE

When a market is trending strongly, this can often be indicated with a trend-line. I use trend lines as a general guide, because they are highly subjective. If you ask 10 different traders to draw a trend line, and you are liable to get 10 different results. Trend lines are drawn beneath the exchange rate in an uptrend, and above the exchange rate in a downtrend (see Figure 9.29).

When the exchange rate is tracking the 10-day EMA, sometimes we can draw a line that is parallel to a trend line; this is referred to as a channel line. A channel line is drawn above the exchange rate in an uptrend and beneath the exchange rate in a downtrend (see Figure 9.30).

Here is one way to take partial exits using this technique: When the exchange rate nears the upper channel line, it is nearing resistance. This means that while the price may continue to rise, it is likely to pull back in the near term.

At the same time, the exchange rate is likely to be extended far away from the moving average. If we entered the trade correctly, we may have been blessed with a significant gain, sometimes in a very short period of time. If this is the case, feel free to use the channel line to take a partial profit.

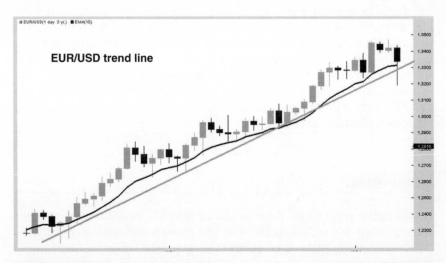

FIGURE 9.29 In an uptrend, the trend line is drawn underneath the exchange rate.

Source: FXtrek IntelliChart™. Copyright © 2001–2006 FXtrek.com, Inc.

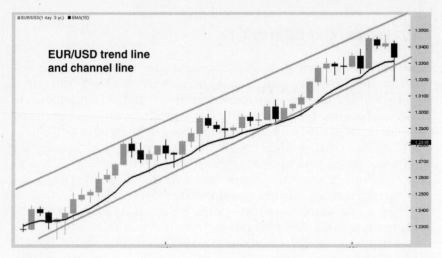

FIGURE 9.30 A channel line is drawn parallel to a trend line, above the exchange rate.

Source: FXtrek IntelliChart™. Copyright © 2001–2006 FXtrek.com, Inc.

Does this mean that we have to wait for the exchange rate to actually touch the channel line before we take our partial exit? No, because trend lines and channel lines are subjective.

Try to look at it this way: Let's assume that we are already profitable by 200 pips on the trade, and the price is just 20 pips away from our channel line. Should we risk our 200-pip gain in order to try to capture those last 20 pips? Since we anticipate that there will be resistance at the channel line, the closer it looms, the more danger for our position.

You can exit *half* of the position at or near the channel line, but you must hold the other half of the trade and trail the stop using the 10-day EMA, as described previously.

RELOADING

It was noted earlier that there might be multiple opportunities to enter a trade using this technique. We can use these additional entry points to "reload" the trade at the appropriate time, using the following rule:

If we have already closed half of the position at or near the channel line, we may replace *that portion* of the trade if the exchange rate falls back to the moving average, creating a new entry point. We may not add a full position; we can only replace the portion of the trade that was closed earlier.

IMPORTANT POINTS TO CONSIDER

In the examples given, all of the trades take place on a daily chart. This is because the trade is based on an important market tendency that deals with the behavior of institutional traders. We have seen evidence that institutions add to positions at the 10-day exponential moving average.

Wishful Thinking

However, there is no evidence that the big players in this market add to positions at the 10-hour moving average, or at the 10-minute moving average. Yet I always encounter traders who try to adapt this system for shorter-term trades. This serves only to render the trade meaningless, as there is absolutely no indication that this style of trading should work in any time frame other than the daily.

The big institutional players tend to be oriented to daily and weekly charts, and are rarely concerned with intraday time frames. They are the ones who are creating support and resistance at the 10-day EMA. Let's not ruin a good technique because we wish it were something other than what it really is.

Correlation

Another important issue is correlation. This issue comes up because a very strong or very weak currency may be involved in several different trending pairs simultaneously. For example, the U.S. dollar may be weak and in a strong downtrend against the euro, the British pound, and the Australian dollar, all at the same time.

When this occurs, we might be tempted to short the U.S. dollar versus those three currencies at the same time, but this would be very dangerous. While it might seem as if we are entering three separate trades, in reality we are creating one huge "short USD" position. If the U.S. dollar then has a strong day, all three of our trades would be lost.

I had one student who shorted the Japanese yen against at least three currencies, because the yen was very weak at the time. The next day, the yen bounced back, and all of his trades were lost. Don't make this dangerous mistake! When we place big bets, either in favor of or against one currency, we are increasing the chances of a large loss.

FINAL THOUGHTS

This technique can be very rewarding, but you may need to be psychologically prepared to work your way through some losing trades in order to get to a big winner. Don't fall into the trap of judging this technique on a few trades, whether they are successful or not. As with any trading technique, the results should be judged over a large sample of trades. In the end, I think you'll find that the FX-Ed Trend Technique a valuable weapon to have in your trading arsenal.

PART III

Nontrending Trading Techniques

Fortunes can be made on trends, but the market does not always co-operate. We need solid techniques for those times when the market is not trending. We can develop these techniques around specific tendencies that are common to the forex market.

CHAPTER 10

The Ultimate Indicator

P eople often ask, what is the best indicator to use in forex trading? Is it the relative strength index (RSI), or exponential moving averages (EMAs), or perhaps Bollinger bands? Or is it something more esoteric? New indicators are being created every day, as market technicians attempt to leave their mark on the trading world. What is the ultimate forex indicator?

Well, there is one indicator that stands above the rest, and that indicator is the price. The price has been and always will be the ultimate indicator. Most indicators are simply an equation or formula that is applied to the price.

THE PRICE IS THE KEY

A moving average is a good example, as it consists of the average, or mean, price of a trading vehicle over a designated period of time. Oscillators such as stochastic or RSI (see Figure 10.1) measure the difference between the current price and recent prices, to determine if a currency pair (or stock, or commodity) is overbought or oversold. Eventually, every indicator boils down to the price.

Technically speaking, in the forex market we do not have a price per se. Instead, we have an exchange rate, which allows us to compare two currencies in one equation. Many times throughout the course of this book, you will notice references to the "price." In currency trading, the word *price* is

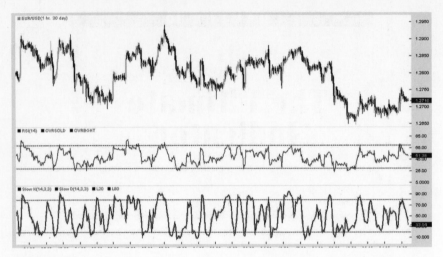

FIGURE 10.1 Oscillators such as RSI and stochastic measure the difference between current and recent prices.

Source: FXtrek IntelliChart™. Copyright © 2001–2006 FXtrek.com, Inc.

simply slang for "exchange rate." This is especially true for those of us who formerly traded stocks, and are in the habit of referring to the numbers that we see on the chart as the "price."

When buyers repeatedly step in at a particular price, this is referred to as support. Think of support as the floor beneath you. If you drop a rubber ball to the floor, it bounces back up to you. The price bounces up from support in a similar fashion.

When sellers repeatedly step in at a particular price, this is referred to as resistance. Think of resistance as the ceiling above you. If you throw a ball at the ceiling, it then falls back down to you. The price falls from resistance in a likewise manner.

Why is this information valuable? Unlike most indicators, support and resistance levels tell us where the buyers and sellers have set up camp. Remember, many of the large players, the hedge funds and the money-center banks, do not enter trades in the same manner that individual traders do.

While many individual traders enter and exit positions all at once, institutional traders usually enter and exit positions gradually. This is necessary due to the large size of the orders being placed. Big traders are concerned that their orders might move the market, by creating too much buying or selling pressure at one time.

In the case of a large buyer, this can drive the exchange rate higher, making additional purchases more expensive. So, instead of chasing the price higher, the institutional trader waits for the price to come back to the

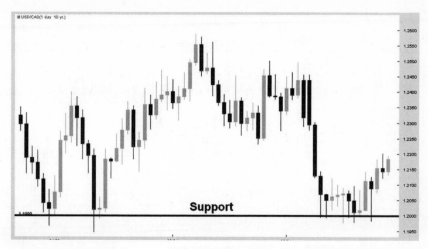

FIGURE 10.2 Support is tested repeatedly in the USD/CAD pair.

Source: FXtrek IntelliChart™. Copyright © 2001–2006 FXtrek.com, Inc.

desired entry point, and then increases the size of the position. The result is a currency pair that bounces back up when it falls to a particular price level (see Figure 10.2).

Conversely, a large seller can inadvertently smash the exchange rate lower, creating an inferior price at which to continue selling. For this reason, the institutional traders will sell at a particular level, wait for the price to rise back up to that level, and then resume selling. The result is a currency pair that tends to stop rising when it reaches a particular price level (see Figure 10.3).

As individual traders, we can use this phenomenon to our advantage. We can enter long trades at the levels where the big traders are buying, and we can sell short at levels where the big traders are selling. We can also exit long trades at points where there is evidence of institutional selling, and exit short trades at points where there is evidence of institutional buying.

It's important that we think of support and resistance as *areas*. In a perfect world, the exchange rate would always rise and fall to the same exact price points, over and over again. The world of trading is far from perfect, and prices rarely rise and fall to the exact same spot.

In the real world, the exchange rate will often overshoot or undershoot the mark (see Figure 10.4). That's why traders using support and resistance should use a "soft target." For example, instead of referring to support as "1.2847," we would consider this to mean that there is support in the area of 1.2850. This is a much more realistic approach to trading support and resistance levels.

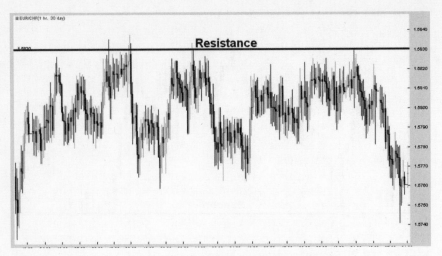

FIGURE 10.3 Resistance forms in the EUR/CHF currency pair.

Source: FXtrek IntelliChart™. Copyright © 2001–2006 FXtrek.com, Inc.

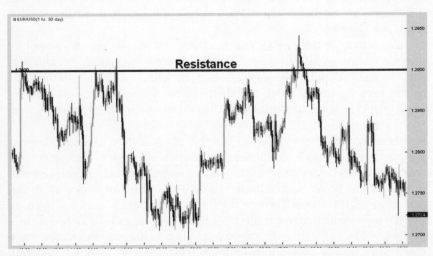

FIGURE 10.4 The EUR/USD exchange rate overshoots and undershoots resistance.

Source: FXtrek IntelliChart™. Copyright © 2001–2006 FXtrek.com, Inc.

WHY SUPPORT BECOMES RESISTANCE

If support and resistance held forever, then trading would be easy indeed. We could simply enter and exit as the price ping-pongs up and down between support and resistance levels. Of course, the idea that trading could be so simple is wishful thinking.

Let's consider the process that occurs when support breaks. Imagine that a support level exists that has withstood numerous tests; in other words, the exchange rate has repeatedly fallen to a price area, only to bounce back up every time. The reason why the price bounces back is that buyers are stepping in at that level on repeated occasions. These buyers could be institutional traders, individual traders, or a combination of the two.

Every time that these traders have entered long positions at the support level, the market has rewarded them; we could say that they've been conditioned by the market to enter at the area of support. One day, the level is tested again, and traders either initiate or add to their long positions.

Only this time the price breaks through, and now traders who entered long at support find that their positions are "under water." Many of these traders will be taken out of their positions by protective stops, which are generally located beneath support for those who are entering long in the area of support. However, since we know that not all traders use stops, some of these individuals will now begin to experience some serious anxiety.

There is a wonderful thing that we can do as we analyze any trading situation: We can try to understand how the situation feels to those who are directly involved. Perhaps at some point in the past, before learning the importance of risk management, we may have been ensnared in a similar predicament as the current market participants described above.

THE PLEASURE PRINCIPLE AND TRADING

You may be familiar with the *pleasure principle*, a psychoanalytical term coined by Gustav Theodor Fechner, a predecessor of Sigmund Freud. Quite simply, the pleasure principle drives one to seek pleasure and to avoid pain. If you can understand this simple concept, and apply it to how you think about trading, it will allow you to understand the reactions of other traders in the market (and you thought Psych 101 was a waste of time!).

The reason for considering the emotions of those involved in the trade is this: Although time passes and traders may come and go, human

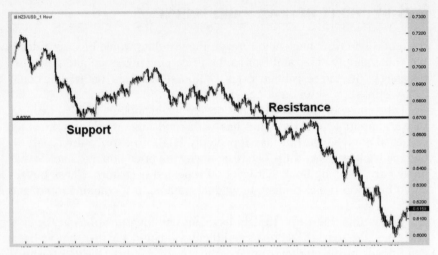

FIGURE 10.5 Former support becomes resistance in the NZD/USD currency pair.

Source: FXtrek IntelliChart™. Copyright © 2001–2006 FXtrek.com, Inc.

nature remains essentially unchanged. Fear and greed have always ruled the markets, and they probably always will.

Now imagine how it must feel for those traders who are holding on to their losing positions after support breaks; what are their predominant emotions? Fear and anxiety immediately come to mind. If these traders are not using good risk management, they are afraid of what might happen next (and they should be afraid!). They are afraid that they may have a big losing trade on their hands, and they are hoping and wishing for the exchange rate to rise.

If the price then rises up near to the entry point (the former support level), many of these traders are going to bail out of their losing trades, so that they can experience a different emotion—a feeling of relief. These traders have but one wish—to get out at or near the breakeven point. Always remember, if at any point during a trade you find yourself hoping or wishing instead of following a predetermined course of action, you should close the trade and reevaluate your trading method.

If enough selling occurs as the price nears the former support level, the exchange rate will reverse and begin to fall. Now, the former area of support has become an area of resistance (see Figure 10.5).

The reverse is also true—a former area of resistance, now broken, can become an area of support for the same reasons (see Figure 10.6).

By the way, we can resolve now that we will never be ensnared in a similar situation, by using good risk management rules such as using a stop

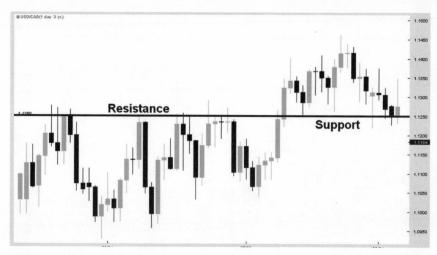

FIGURE 10.6　Former resistance becomes support in the USD/CAD currency pair.

Source: FXtrek IntelliChart™. Copyright © 2001–2006 FXtrek.com, Inc.

on every trade, and by never averaging down on a losing trade. Traders who do not use stops and average down on losing trades are not really traders at all—at least, they won't be for long.

PRICE ACTION

Traders are not only concerned with the ability (or lack thereof) of the price to break through support or resistance, but are also concerned with the behavior of the price when it reaches these key levels. They want to know not only *if* support or resistance is holding, but also *how* it is holding.

For example, did the price make a half-hearted attempt at breaching support, and then drift away, or did it fail repeatedly in its persistent attempts to break out to the other side?

How is the price moving? Is it rushing headlong toward support or resistance, indicating a strong commitment on the part of traders? Or is it meandering aimlessly, as if traders were afraid of encountering a key level?

The "attitude" of the price at key support and resistance levels can betray the next directional move. I never want to enter a trade based on support or resistance unless I can first observe the price action.

For example, if a pair repeatedly fails after numerous attempts to breach resistance, it reveals the presence of a large seller in the vicinity.

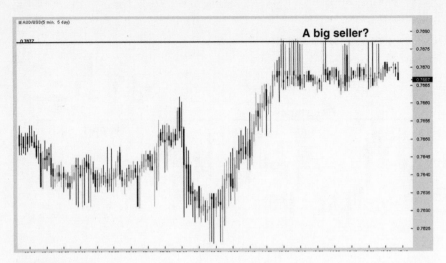

FIGURE 10.7 Repeated failure to breach resistance; is a large seller in the vicinity?

Source: FXtrek IntelliChart™. Copyright © 2001–2006 FXtrek.com, Inc.

I can "lean" on this seller, meaning that I will join him in selling this pair at resistance (see Figure 10.7).

The point is that this seller may be building or exiting a large position; either way, he might continue selling for some time. If the price finally breaks resistance, I would interpret this to mean that the seller is finished, and the order is filled. There would no longer be any reason to place trades based on that resistance level. Remember, if the reason for entering the trade is no longer valid, then the trade itself is no longer valid.

DON'T STAND IN FRONT OF A FREIGHT TRAIN

Many traders make the mistake of placing an order directly on a support or resistance level, and then waiting. This removes any chance for the trader to use the chart's price action to his or her advantage.

Placing an order in this manner is similar to making a prediction that the level will hold, but this is not advisable. No matter how dependable that support or resistance level has been in the past, it can and often will break. If the price is rushing headlong toward your support or resistance level, get out of the way.

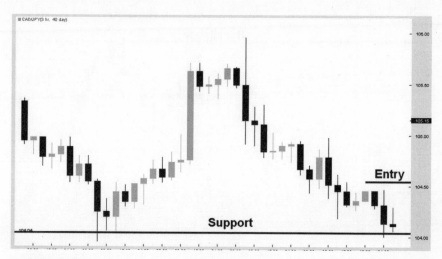

FIGURE 10.8 As the exchange rate falls to support, place the entry order above support.

Source: FXtrek IntelliChart™. Copyright © 2001–2006 FXtrek.com, Inc.

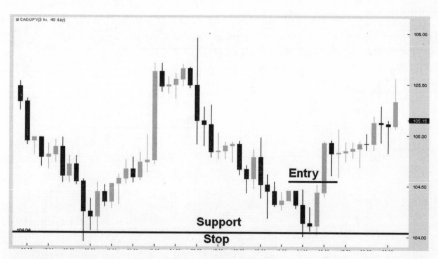

FIGURE 10.9 The stop is placed beneath support.

Source: FXtrek IntelliChart™. Copyright © 2001–2006 FXtrek.com, Inc.

FIGURE 10.10 As the exchange rate rises to resistance, place the entry beneath resistance.

Source: FXtrek IntelliChart™. Copyright © 2001–2006 FXtrek.com, Inc.

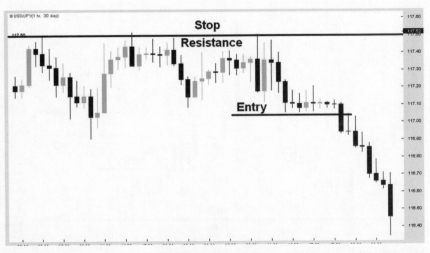

FIGURE 10.11 The stop is placed above resistance.

Source: FXtrek IntelliChart™. Copyright © 2001–2006 FXtrek.com, Inc.

We want some measure of assurance that support will hold. Instead of trying to catch a long entry as the price is falling, try this: Allow the price to fall to support, and then set up an entry order to go long, above support. Wait until the price is beneath you, testing support, and only *then* place the entry order (see Figure 10.8). Your stop will be located beneath support (see Figure 10.9).

When the price reaches support, one of two things will happen: Either the price will keep falling, or it will turn and begin to rise. If the price keeps falling, we haven't lost a thing, because our entry order has not been reached. But if the price bounces up, we now have evidence of buying at the support level.

The idea is to catch the entry for the long trade as the price is rising from support. Sure, we will not be able to enter the trade at the bottom of support, but that's ok. We want to increase our chances of success by waiting until the evidence is on our side.

In the case of resistance, we can simply do the opposite; allow the exchange rate to rise up to resistance, and then place your entry order beneath resistance (see Figure 10.10). Your stop will be located above resistance. This way, if the resistance level holds, we can catch the currency pair as the price is falling. If the level fails and the price breaks higher, our order will remain unexecuted (see Figure 10.11).

CHAPTER 11

Keys to Intraday Breakouts

When trading intraday breakouts, or when engaging in any type of trading, for that matter, it is important for the trader to use every type of advantage possible. We want to search for situations in which the odds are in our favor, and then take action.

In all forms of trading, no matter if the vehicle is in the equity, futures, or forex market, there are many instances of false breakouts. A false breakout occurs when the price appears to break below support or above resistance, only to rise back above support or fall back below resistance.

In order to reduce the negative effects of these false breakouts, and to improve our chances of success, let's take a closer look at intraday breakouts and how to trade them.

ASCENDING AND DESCENDING TRIANGLES

Ascending and descending triangles create excellent intraday breakout opportunities, because the pattern itself establishes a directional bias for the currency pair. An ascending triangle is formed by a combination of diagonal support and horizontal resistance (Figure 11.1), while a descending triangle is formed by a combination of diagonal resistance and horizontal support (Figure 11.2).

In the case of an ascending triangle, the bulls are gaining strength and buying at higher and higher levels, while the bears are merely trying to defend an established level of resistance. Since the bulls are more aggressive

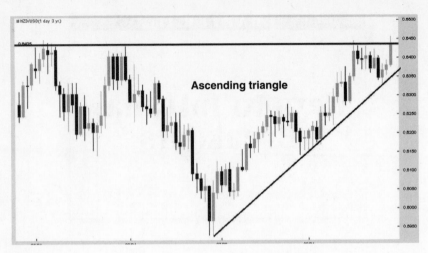

FIGURE 11.1 Ascending triangle forms in the NZD/USD currency pair.

Source: FXtrek IntelliChart™. Copyright © 2001–2006 FXtrek.com, Inc.

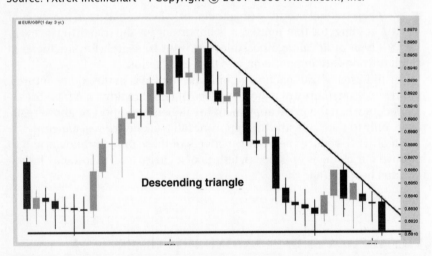

FIGURE 11.2 Descending triangle forms in the EUR/GBP currency pair.

Source: FXtrek IntelliChart™. Copyright © 2001–2006 FXtrek.com, Inc.

than the bears, they are more likely to prevail in this battle. The odds favor a breakout to the upside.

In the case of a descending triangle, the bears are gaining strength and selling at lower and lower levels, while the bulls are merely trying to defend an established level of support. The bears are the more aggressive party in this case, so the odds favor a breakout to the downside.

TREND FILTER

While it is helpful to know that the odds are in our favor, we can increase our edge and take it to the next level. When trading ascending or descending triangles, the trader can gain a further edge by checking the direction of the currency pair prior to the formation of the triangle pattern.

This is because it's not unusual for a currency pair to trend in one direction, then consolidate, and then resume trending in the same direction. The directional bias of an ascending or descending triangle favors a break of horizontal support or resistance. If the pair was trending in the same direction prior to the formation of the triangle pattern, the trade becomes all the more compelling.

For example, on the hourly chart of the EUR/JPY pair, we see the formation of an ascending triangle (see Figure 11.3). The first thing the trader needs to ask is: What was the direction of the trend (if any) prior to the formation of the triangle?

If we take a longer view of the pair (Figure 11.4), we can see that the pair has been trending steadily higher. It's important that we use the power of this trend to our advantage, to reduce the occurrence of false breakouts and increase our chances of success.

By filtering our breakout trades in this manner, we are once again incorporating the trend into our techniques. As a general rule, traders should

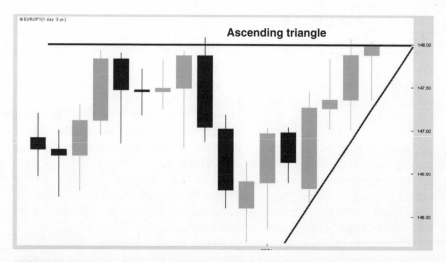

FIGURE 11.3 An ascending triangle forms in the EUR/JPY currency pair.

Source: FXtrek IntelliChart™. Copyright © 2001–2006 FXtrek.com, Inc.

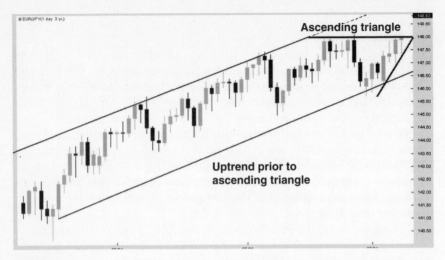

FIGURE 11.4 Prior to the formation of the ascending triangle, the pair was in an uptrend.

Source: FXtrek IntelliChart™. Copyright © 2001–2006 FXtrek.com, Inc.

always trade with the trend, and never fight the trend. It is essentially the difference between swimming with the tide or against the tide, and traders who fight against trends often regret their actions.

TIME-OF-DAY FILTER

Another edge that we can put to use when trading intraday breakouts is the time of day. Perhaps you are familiar with the trading axiom that a breakout is considered to be significant if it occurs on high volume, and is considered less reliable if it occurs on low volume.

This is because it takes "real money" to generate a move that occurs on high volume. In a high-volume environment, the move is considered real because the players are putting significant amounts of capital to work—if they weren't, the currency pair wouldn't budge.

In a low-volume environment, orders that normally wouldn't have a significant impact on exchange rates now have the ability to move markets. Banks and institutions realize this, and may attempt to give the exchange rate a little "push" during times of low volume.

By applying buying or selling pressure at the right time, these institutional traders can cause pools of orders to be executed, and thus generate commissions. This is much easier to do when volume is light, and the move tends to be very brief.

While forex traders are not able to easily access accurate volume figures, we do know that trading is not equally liquid at all times of the day, and there are certainly some times of day that generate more volume than others.

For example, since we know that the London session has the highest volume, we'll consider breakouts that occur during this session to be legitimate. We would especially consider these breakouts to be significant if they occur early in the session, as this is the time of day that normally generates the highest volume and the greatest liquidity.

On the other hand, volume tends to lessen at certain times of the trading day. For example, if a breakout were to occur late in the Asian trading session, or late in the U.S. trading session, that breakout would be considered suspect. Chances are the move is occurring on light volume, and this increases the likelihood of a false breakout.

Just like an equity trader, we'll assume that a breakout that occurs at a time of high volume is legitimate, and a breakout that occurs at a time of low volume is suspect. Remember, although we cannot see the actual volume figures, we do know which times of day generate the most volume.

For example, let's take a look at the daily chart of EUR/USD (Figure 11.5). The pair had formed strong support in the summer of 2004 at 1.2000, which is also a number that takes on added psychological significance because it is a large round number.

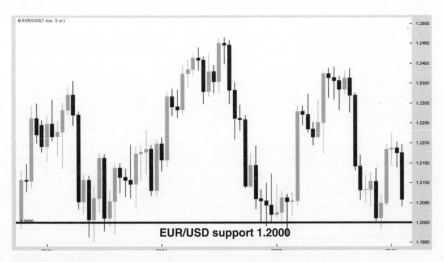

FIGURE 11.5 EUR/USD—Major support forms at the round number 1.2000.

Source: FXtrek IntelliChart™. Copyright © 2001–2006 FXtrek.com, Inc.

FIGURE 11.6 EUR/USD returns to 1.2000 support area in 2005.

Source: FXtrek IntelliChart™. Copyright © 2001–2006 FXtrek.com, Inc.

In fact, the pair could not close below 1.2000 for quite some time. After numerous failed attempts to break the support level, the pair drifted higher. Eventually, it returned to the same area of support in the summer of 2005, when it cautiously hovered near 1.2000 (see Figure 11.6).

Finally, during the June 24 session, the pair suddenly tries to break support. However, we can see in the five-minute chart (Figure 11.7) that the break was short-lived, a classic example of a false breakout.

A trader who paid attention to the time of day would have noted that the break occurred late in the Asian session and prior to the London session, a time of day that is notorious for low volume and for false breakouts.

Such a trader would have considered the timing of this event to be suspicious and would have refrained from entering a trade in the direction of the breakout. In fact, if a breakout does occur during a low-volume time of day, it would be acceptable to "fade" – or trade against – the breakout. In other words, the trader is assuming that the low-volume breakout will fail.

One week later, on July 1, the pair tried to break the support level once again, only this time the breakout occurred at approximately 14:30 GMT (see Figure 11.8). At this time of day, the London session is ongoing, and the New York session is well under way.

As a result, this is a time of high volume and the breakout is more likely to succeed. This time, the breakout is real. The pair finally breaks 1.2000, and drifts as low as 1.1865 over the next few days.

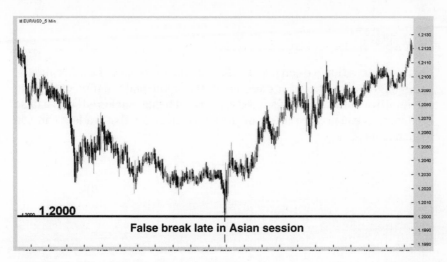

FIGURE 11.7 EUR/USD—Brief break below support occurs late in the Asian session.

Source: FXtrek IntelliChart™. Copyright © 2001–2006 FXtrek.com, Inc.

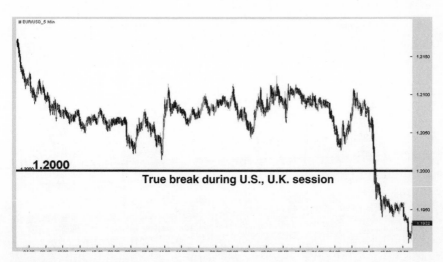

FIGURE 11.8 EUR/USD—True break occurs as the U.K. and U.S. sessions overlap.

Source: FXtrek IntelliChart™. Copyright © 2001–2006 FXtrek.com, Inc.

SUMMARY

There are steps that we can take to alleviate the problem of false breakouts. By using triangles, the prior direction of the trend, and the time of day, we can improve our chances of success and avoid being "suckered" into a false breakout. These are just a few of the subtle nuances that traders can use to gain an edge.

CHAPTER 12

Flags and Pennants

I magine that you must climb 10 flights of stairs as quickly as possible. You dash up the first five flights of stairs, and then stop to catch your breath. After this short pause, you resume bounding up the staircase toward the tenth floor.

Are we preparing for the Olympics or a triathlon? No, this type of behavior actually relates to a trading phenomenon. It's not unusual for the exchange rate of a currency pair to race higher, then pause, and then continue to climb. Similarly, we often see the price fall rapidly, then consolidate, and then continue its descent.

This period of "rest" is called a consolidation. We say that a currency pair (or stock, or commodity) consolidates its gains (or losses) before moving on. A consolidation that indicates that the exchange rate will resume moving in its previous direction is called a continuation pattern.

Flags and pennants are short-term continuation patterns; after the formation of one of these patterns, the exchange rate has a tendency to continue moving in the same direction as it was prior to the consolidation. These patterns are generally found on short-term or intraday charts.

In the case of a flag or a pennant, the initial move is a sudden, sharp directional thrust. It doesn't matter if the move is an advance or a decline, what matters is the velocity of the move. This sharp burst creates a long candle or a series of long candles on our short-term chart, and is referred to as a *flagpole*. If the movement is not sharp or sudden, the reliability of the pattern is called into question. The sharp movement, either higher or lower, is what gives the formation its meaning.

153

PENNANTS

Figure 12.1 shows an example of a pennant formation in the euro/U.S. dollar currency pair. A sharp thrust higher creates the flagpole, and then the exchange rate begins to consolidate into a symmetrical triangle. This is the pause before the potential breakout. As the price clears the top of the pennant, the signal for a long entry is given. Let's take a look at the specific details of this formation and a technique for using it to place winning trades.

Pennants involve two parts: a nearly vertical flagpole and a triangular consolidation. The consolidation is very much like a symmetrical triangle, but shorter in duration. The symmetrical triangle implies that traders feel comfortable with the current exchange rate. However, the pennant is a continuation pattern, meaning that any sense of comfort or a "truce" between the bulls and the bears is likely to be short lived.

The first step to trading the formation is to measure the flagpole (see Figure 12.2). In this case, the flagpole is a single long candle, and has a range of 100 pips from low to high (the low of the candle is 1.2727, the high is 1.2827).

Next, as the exchange rate consolidates into a triangle, we'll determine the entry point for our prospective trade. In order to do this, we'll calculate an amount equal to 10 percent of the height of the flagpole. In this case, 10 percent would be equal to 10 pips (the height of the flagpole = 100 pips; 10 percent of 100 pips = 10 pips).

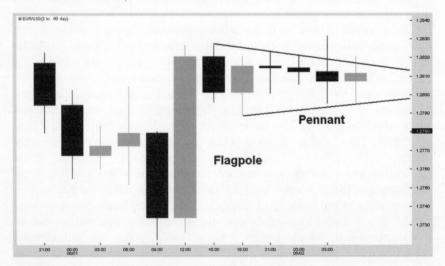

FIGURE 12.1 A pennant formation in the EUR/USD currency pair.

Source: FXtrek IntelliChart™. Copyright © 2001–2006 FXtrek.com, Inc.

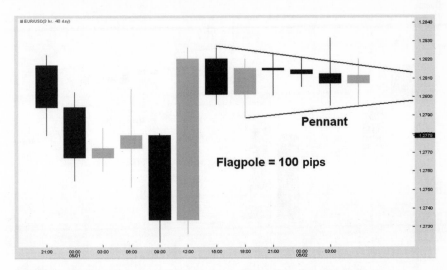

FIGURE 12.2 The flagpole is measured to calculate the entry and stop.

Source: FXtrek IntelliChart™. Copyright © 2001–2006 FXtrek.com, Inc.

Then, we'll place our entry order above the high point of the flagpole. Since the high point of the flagpole is 1.2827, we'll simply add 10 percent (in this case, 10 pips) to the top of the flagpole, giving us an entry point of 1.2837 (see Figure 12.3).

Of course, if we do enter a trade, we'll need to place a stop. The stop is calculated by using a number of pips that is equivalent to 25 percent of the flagpole. So, since the height of the flagpole is 100 pips, the stop will be placed 25 pips below the entry point (see Figure 12.4). Please note that the stop is 25 pips beneath the entry point, not 25 pips below the top of the flagpole. Since the entry point is 1.2837, we'll subtract 25 pips from 1.2837, which places our stop at 1.2812.

Finally, we will need to create exits for our trade. Our first target will be equal to the amount of pips (per lot) that we are risking on the trade. So, since our risk per lot is 25 pips, we can exit half of the position when we are profitable by 25 pips. This will place our first exit at 1.2862 (1.2837 plus 25 pips = 1.2862).

Managing the Trade

The second target will be equal to the approximate distance from the beginning of the flagpole to the pennant (the length of the flagpole). Since the flagpole measured 100 pips from top to bottom, the target will be 100 pips above the top of the flagpole. This will give us our second exit at 1.2927—a potential gain of 90 pips. It's important to note that we add the 100 pips

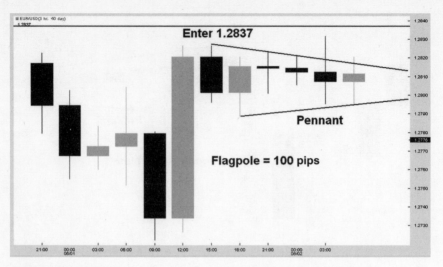

FIGURE 12.3   The entry point is above the flagpole and the pennant.

Source: FXtrek IntelliChart™. Copyright © 2001–2006 FXtrek.com, Inc.

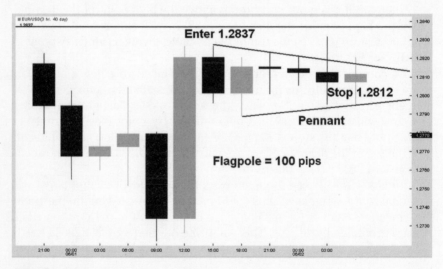

FIGURE 12.4   The stop is calculated.

Source: FXtrek IntelliChart™. Copyright © 2001–2006 FXtrek.com, Inc.

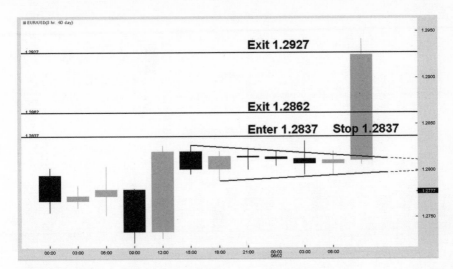

FIGURE 12.5 Exits are created; entry and exits are triggered.

Source: FXtrek IntelliChart™. Copyright © 2001–2006 FXtrek.com, Inc.

to the top of the flagpole (1.2827), *not* to the entry point (1.2837). (see Figure 12.5).

If and when the exchange rate reaches the first exit of 1.2862, we will raise our stop to our entry point of 1.2837. This will eliminate any remaining risk from the trade, and creates a worst-case scenario of a 25-pip profit on the first portion of the trade, and a "scratch" (breakeven) on the second part of the trade.

In this example, the currency pair experiences a strong initial thrust, creating a flagpole. Then, the pair consolidates into a pennant formation, indicating that traders are temporarily uncertain, and that the bulls and bears have "called a truce." You can see that the upper wick of one of the candles pops through the top of the pennant, but doesn't go far enough to trigger an entry at 1.2837.

Two candles later, the upward movement returns with a vengeance, triggering our entry at 1.2837 and, shortly thereafter, our first exit at 1.2862. Before the candle is completed, the exchange rate reaches a high of 1.2941, more than enough to achieve our second exit of 1.2927.

The Effect of News

Here is another example; in this situation, after the U.S. Federal Reserve released a "dovish" statement on monetary policy (leading traders to believe that they might not raise interest rates), the U.S. dollar plunged against

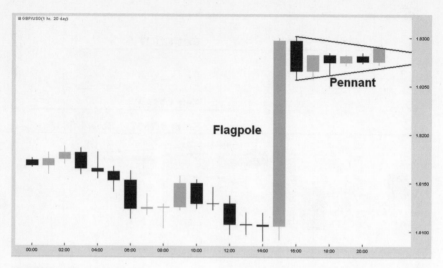

FIGURE 12.6 GBP/USD currency pair spikes higher by about 200 pips, forms pennant.

Source: FXtrek IntelliChart™. Copyright © 2001–2006 FXtrek.com, Inc.

most major currencies, including the British pound. As a result, the Great Britain Pound/U.S. Dollar (GBP/USD) currency pair immediately spiked higher by about 200 pips, starting at 1.8100 and topping out at about 1.8300 (see Figure 12.6).

This sudden change in the exchange rate attracted sellers, who no doubt believed that "what goes up must come down." Of course we know that this is not necessarily the case, as the law of gravity does not hold sway over any trading market. As the buyers and sellers achieved temporary equilibrium, a pennant formation occurred.

The mind of the currency trader immediately calculates that since the flagpole is 200 pips in length, the entry point will be above the top of the flagpole by a number of pips equal to 10 percent of 200 pips. Therefore, our potential entry point is 20 pips above the top of the flagpole, at 1.8320 (see Figure 12.7). This will help us to avoid any false breaks out of the pennant.

Next, the trader calculates that the stop must be equal to 25 percent of the flagpole. Twenty-five percent of 200 pips gives us 50 pips, so our stop will be located at 1.8270, or 50 pips below the entry point of 1.8320 (see Figure 12.8). If the breakout should fail, the exchange rate will fall back into the pennant formation, and we will be stopped out of the trade with a loss.

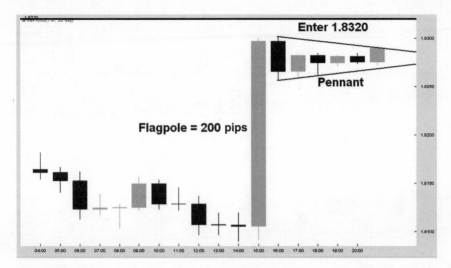

FIGURE 12.7 The entry order is placed above the flagpole and pennant.

Source: FXtrek IntelliChart™. Copyright © 2001–2006 FXtrek.com, Inc.

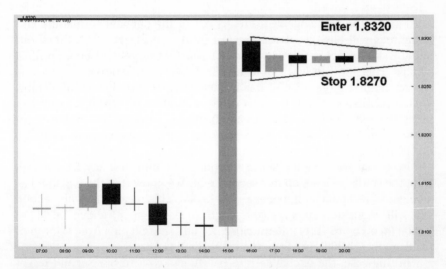

FIGURE 12.8 The stop is calculated. This is done before the trade is entered.

Source: FXtrek IntelliChart™. Copyright © 2001–2006 FXtrek.com, Inc.

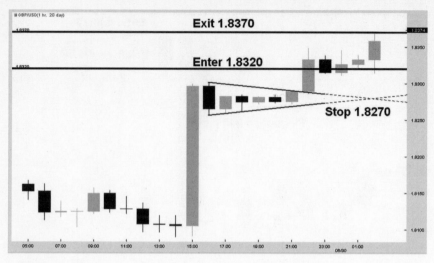

FIGURE 12.9 The initial target has a 1:1 risk-reward ratio.

Source: FXtrek IntelliChart™. Copyright © 2001–2006 FXtrek.com, Inc.

Finally, the exchange rate breaks out of the pennant formation. Our initial exit will have a 1:1 risk-reward ratio (see Figure 12.9). Since our initial risk is equal to 50 pips (per lot), our first target will be a profit of 50 pips. This puts our first exit at 1.8370 (1.8320 plus 50 pips).

As the first target of 1.8370 is hit, we'll take a partial profit of 50 pips. We'll also raise our stop from its original location of 1.8270 to our entry point of 1.8320, which eliminates any further risk on the remainder of our position, and gives us a worst-case scenario of a profitable trade (see Figure 12.10).

Now that we have locked in a profit and eliminated any further risk from the trade, let's set up our second exit. We know that the flagpole has a height of 200 pips, and its peak was 1.8300. This means that our second exit will be located 200 pips (the length of the flagpole) above 1.8300, at 1.8500 (see Figure 12.11). Remember, we add the 200 pips from the top of the flagpole (1.8300), not from the entry point (1.8320).

In this case, the exchange rate barely makes it to our second target before sliding back. Even if the second exit had not been achieved, we still managed to protect ourselves by locking in a gain with a partial profit, and eliminated any further risk by raising the stop. This leaves a worst-case scenario of a profitable trade, which is exactly the type of situation that we want.

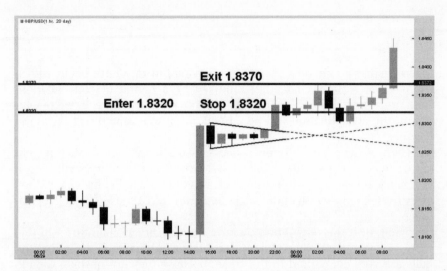

FIGURE 12.10 The stop is raised as the first exit is achieved. A partial profit is taken.

Source: FXtrek IntelliChart™. Copyright © 2001–2006 FXtrek.com, Inc.

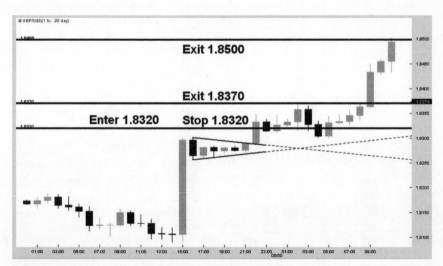

FIGURE 12.11 The exchange rate rallies to the second exit.

Source: FXtrek IntelliChart™. Copyright © 2001–2006 FXtrek.com, Inc.

FLAGS

Flag formations are very similar to pennants, in that both begin with a sharp move (called a flagpole) followed by a period of consolidation. Both are also continuation patterns, meaning that the most likely resolution of the consolidation will be a breakout in the same direction as the flagpole.

Here is the main difference between a pennant and a flag: a pennant consists of two lines that slope toward each other (similar to a symmetrical triangle), while a flag consists of two parallel lines that slope away from the direction of the flagpole. Figure 12.12 shows the flag formation.

Think of it this way: First, there is a sharp directional move—in this case, a move higher. We could interpret this sharp move to mean that the bulls are very committed to the trade, because they are pushing the exchange rate higher in an aggressive manner. They are likely buying in quantity, without much regard for the price they are paying.

Next, the bears get their chance to fight back. We can see that the bears are only able to bring the exchange rate down moderately and slowly—in fact, they are not as aggressive as the bulls, and are not exerting nearly as much selling pressure on the currency pair. The bulls clearly have the

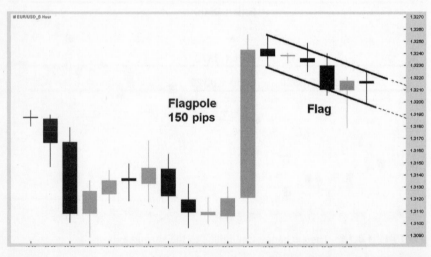

FIGURE 12.12 A flag consists of two parallel lines that slope away from the flag-pole.

Source: FXtrek IntelliChart™. Copyright © 2001–2006 FXtrek.com, Inc.

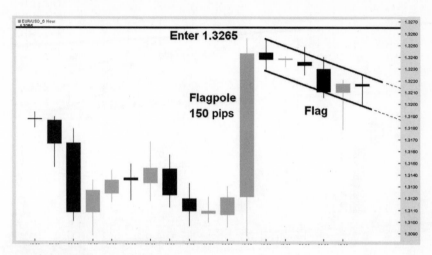

FIGURE 12.13 The flagpole is measured to calculate the entry point.

Source: FXtrek IntelliChart™. Copyright © 2001–2006 FXtrek.com, Inc.

upper hand and are acting on their conviction that the exchange rate should rise, while the bears are much less certain of their position in the market.

Since the bulls are more aggressive and have greater conviction in this case, they are more likely to keep on buying. The bears are more likely to be the "weak hands" and are liable to bail out of their positions more quickly, since they have less at stake.

Flags are traded in a manner that is very similar to the method used to trade pennants. First, we measure the flagpole, which has a height of about 150 pips, beginning at 1.3100 and topping out at about 1.3250 (see Figure 12.13). Our entry will be at a point above the flagpole, by an amount equal to 10 percent of the flagpole. Since 10 percent of 150 pips = 15 pips, we will place our entry order at 1.3265, which is 15 pips above the top of the flagpole.

Next, the stop must be calculated; the stop will be placed a number of pips equal to 25 percent of the height of the flagpole. Since the height of the flagpole in this case is 150 pips, and 25 percent of 150 = 37.5 (we can round it up to 38 pips), our stop will be located at 1.3227 (1.3265 minus 38 pips = 1.3227). See Figure 12.14. Note that the stop is 38 pips below the entry point, not 38 pips below the top of the flagpole. By using this method to create our stop, our account is protected in the event of a false breakout.

Several candles later, our entry is triggered and the exchange rate is rushing higher. Just as we did with the pennant formation, our first exit

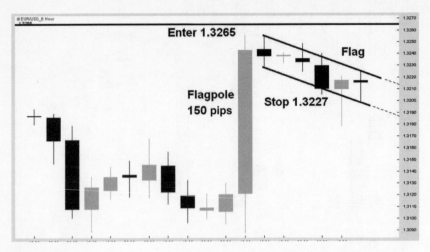

FIGURE 12.14   The stop is calculated in a manner similar to the pennant formation.

Source: FXtrek IntelliChart™. Copyright © 2001–2006 FXtrek.com, Inc.

will be equal to the amount of risk we are taking on a "per lot" basis. Since we are risking 38 pips per lot, our first exit will be located 38 pips above our entry point. Let's add 38 pips to our entry point of 1.3265, giving us our first exit at 1.3303 (see Figure 12.15).

When the first exit of 1.3303 is reached, we will take a partial profit of 38 pips, and at the same time we will raise the stop to eliminate any further risk from the trade (see Figure 12.16). Our worst-case scenario is now a 38-pip profit on the first part of the trade, and a break-even trade on the second portion.

Now that we have locked in a profit and eliminated any additional risk, let's set up our second exit. We know that the flagpole had a height of 150 pips, and it peaked at 1.3250. This means that our second exit will be located 150 pips above 1.3250, at 1.3400 (see Figure 12.17).

We can see that in this case, the EUR/USD exchange rate easily reaches our first target, and then gradually climbs to achieve the second target. Trading in this manner on a consistent basis keeps risk in check and losses within reason, and creates large winning trades in comparison to the size of the losing trades.

FILTERING ENTRIES

Like any pattern, strategy, or technique, flags and pennants are not fool-proof. Here is a flag pattern that occurs on the EUR/USD 10-minute

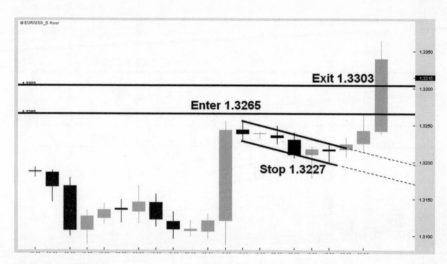

FIGURE 12.15 The first exit equals the amount of risk taken on a "per lot" basis.
Source: FXtrek IntelliChart™. Copyright © 2001–2006 FXtrek.com, Inc.

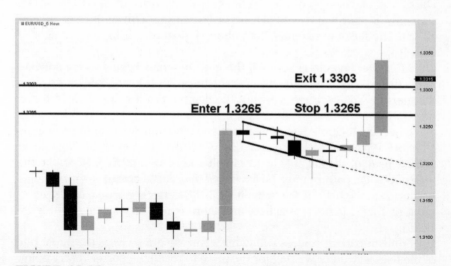

FIGURE 12.16 First exit is reached; partial profit is taken and the stop is raised.
Source: FXtrek IntelliChart™. Copyright © 2001–2006 FXtrek.com, Inc.

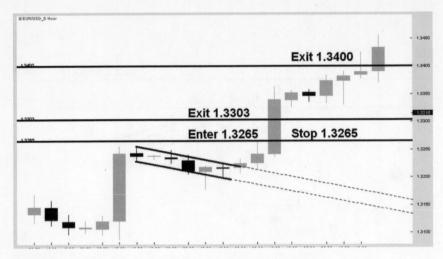

FIGURE 12.17 The exchange rate reaches the second exit.

Source: FXtrek IntelliChart™. Copyright © 2001–2006 FXtrek.com, Inc.

chart. We can see that the exchange rate is drifting sideways, when suddenly a sharp move higher occurs, creating a flagpole (see Figure 12.18). The flagpole extends from about 1.2820 to 1.2940, for a height of 120 pips.

After the flagpole is formed, the currency pair begins to consolidate into a flag pattern. The exchange rate begins to drift lower, and as we draw the lines into place, the borders of the flag pattern are apparent (see Figure 12.19).

Since the flagpole has a height of 120 pips, our point of entry will be 12 pips (10 percent of 120 pips = 12 pips) above the top of the flagpole, at 1.2952 (peak of the flagpole at 1.2940 plus 12 pips = 1.2952). Note that the high of the flag pattern must be exceeded in order to create an entry signal. In this case, the high of the flagpole (1.2940) is never cleared, so the entry point of 1.2952 is never reached, and there is no entry signal (see Figure 12.20).

Some impatient traders will enter when the price clears the upper line of the flag, instead of waiting for the price to reach the correct entry point. This would be a mistake; if the exchange rate escapes from the flag formation but fails to clear the top of the flagpole, there is no reason to believe that the trade should be successful. By waiting for the exchange rate to clear the top of the pattern by an amount equal to 10 percent of the flag, we have filtered out an inferior entry that would have failed.

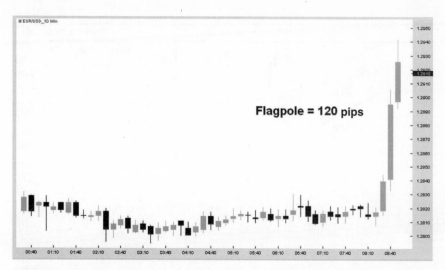

FIGURE 12.18 A flagpole forms as the exchange rate rockets higher.

Source: FXtrek IntelliChart™. Copyright © 2001–2006 FXtrek.com, Inc.

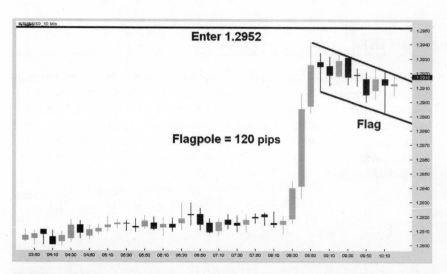

FIGURE 12.19 The flagpole is measured and the entry point is calculated.

Source: FXtrek IntelliChart™. Copyright © 2001–2006 FXtrek.com, Inc.

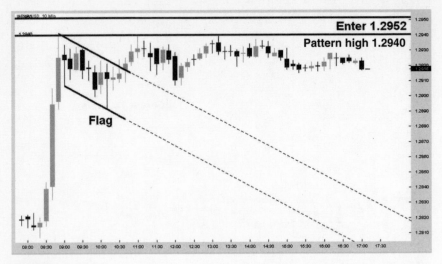

FIGURE 12.20 The exchange rate fails to reach the entry point. No trade is entered.

Source: FXtrek IntelliChart™. Copyright © 2001–2006 FXtrek.com, Inc.

SUMMARY

Remember, the idea behind this technique (or any technique) is not to place the most trades; it is to place the best trades. Many traders become impatient and enter trades even though the proper criteria have not been met. In this case, and in many others, their eagerness to "pull the trigger" will work against them. Patience and discipline, and the ability to follow a trading plan, will help us to avoid falling into this trap, and keep us on course for trading success.

CHAPTER 13

The Squeeze Play

A s we noted earlier, most good trading strategies begin with a market tendency; traders notice that the market tends to behave in a certain way, and then they create a strategy that seeks to capitalize on this tendency. Let's look at a strategy that is designed to take advantage of volatility in the forex market.

THE CYCLE OF VOLATILITY

Volatility tends to run in cycles. In other words, periods of high volatility tend to be followed by periods of low volatility. There is a simple explanation for this; when a market is trending, as the forex market often does, the participants have a definite opinion as to the direction of the trade.

This cycle can be observed in almost any trading market, but it's most closely identified with options trading. Options traders write put and call contracts during periods of high volatility, to collect the "premium"—the cost of the contract. The premiums attached to these contracts tend to be fatter when markets are volatile.

The option writer assumes volatility will return to normal levels in the future, allowing him to buy back the contracts at a reduced premium. In the world of options, this concept is referred to as *selling volatility*. This cycle of volatility can also be observed in the forex market.

PERCEPTION MOVES THE MARKET

When a currency pair begins to trend, traders are showing a strong preference for one currency over another. During strong trends, the market is volatile because the price is on the move. The perception of value has changed, and the price must move to reflect this change of opinion.

After the trend has continued for a while, the currency pair will reach a point where the participants feel that the exchange rate is fairly valued. There will come a point when the bulls and the bears reach an agreement—at least temporarily—that a currency pair is reasonably priced.

At this point, the trend pauses and the pair enters a period of consolidation. The price settles into a narrow range, as there is no real reason for the exchange rate to break out one way or the other. The period of consolidation may be brief or lengthy.

Eventually, this period of consolidation must end. The bulls and bears may have reached a temporary truce, but eventually new information will be introduced into the market, and the perception of the value of the currency pair will change as this news is digested.

Economic indicators are often the catalyst for this change of opinion. Unexpected news events can cause the exchange rate to break out of its narrow consolidation, and run until the price reaches a new area where the bulls and bears are once again able to reach a temporary truce.

Fundamentals Influence Volatility

For example, during the spring and early summer of 2005, many issues led to a negative perception of the euro. These included the European Union's failure to pass a constitution and failure to reach a budget agreement.

Additionally, European nations were hobbled by slow economic growth and high unemployment. European interest rates appeared poised to move lower, in order to stimulate these economies.

As many experienced currency traders are well aware, lower interest rates tend to cause the underlying currency to weaken, because fixed-income investors want the best possible yields for their investments. These investors will often pull their funds out of a country to find more attractive yields in another part of the world.

This creates a flow of funds out of the nations that are lowering interest rates (or are perceived to be lowering rates in the future), causing the underlying currency (in this case the euro) to weaken. Investors sold the euro in anticipation of this potential decrease in interest rates.

Euro and U.S. Dollar Fundamentals

At the same time that European nations were experiencing these difficulties, the United States was enjoying relatively strong growth and an improving employment picture.

The U.S. Federal Reserve was in the midst of a campaign of rate hikes, which have the effect of strengthening the U.S. dollar by making U.S.-denominated bonds and other fixed-income instruments more attractive to overseas investors. This creates a flow of capital into a country that offers high-yielding investments, which strengthens the underlying currency (in this case the U.S. dollar).

Because U.S. interest rates at that time were higher than European rates, traders who were long the U.S. dollar and short the euro were able to earn interest on the trade, in addition to any capital appreciation.

Conversely, traders who were long the euro versus the U.S. dollar would have to pay interest. At the time, it seemed that there were plenty of good reasons to buy the greenback, but few compelling reasons to own the euro.

These events gave traders a strong opinion as to the relative value of these two currencies, and traders mercilessly dumped the euro in favor of the U.S. dollar. The euro/U.S. dollar exchange rate fell sharply, from nearly 1.35 on March 11 to below 1.19 on July 5, a plunge of nearly 1,600 pips.

By mid-July, traders apparently felt that the euro had been punished enough, and by late summer the pair settled into a period of relatively directionless and narrow trading. It was time to start looking for a volatility breakout setup.

Moving Averages and Volatility

Many traders use moving averages as an indication of volatility. In Figure 13.1, we see that the 20-day exponential moving average (EMA) is sloping sharply downward during the trending phase.

As the pair consolidates in late summer, the 20-day EMA is moving in a relatively flat and sideways manner. The flat 20-day exponential moving average is one indication that the trend has paused, at least temporarily, and the price has entered the consolidation phase.

Additional Indicators for Confirmation

In order to confirm that this consolidation represents a trade setup, we'll refer to two additional indicators (see Figure 13.2). Simply put, these two

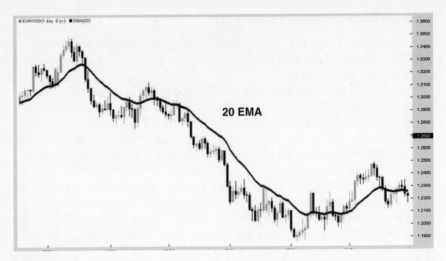

FIGURE 13.1 The 20-period EMA turns sharply downward during the trending phase.

Source: FXtrek IntelliChart™. Copyright © 2001–2006 FXtrek.com, Inc.

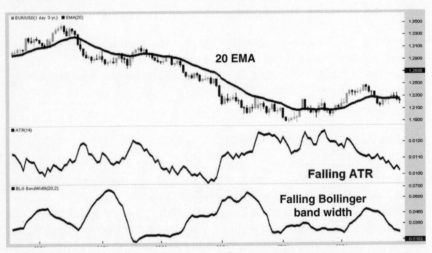

FIGURE 13.2 ATR and Bollinger band width confirming that volatility is falling.

Source: FXtrek IntelliChart™. Copyright © 2001–2006 FXtrek.com, Inc.

indicators are specifically designed to measure volatility. If the indicators are falling, volatility is falling. Once volatility contracts, the currency pair has settled in for a period of consolidation, which could lead to a powerful breakout.

The first of these indicators is average true range (ATR), which is a measurement of the average trading range of a currency pair over a given period of time. In this case, we are measuring the range based on the daily chart, using the default parameter of 14 periods. As we can see, the ATR indicator is falling, meaning that the average daily range is shrinking, and volatility is decreasing.

Bollinger bands also measure volatility. Bollinger bands split open when volatility is high and converge when volatility falls. Instead of using the bands themselves, we can use the Bollinger band width indicator, which is simply a measure of the space between the Bollinger bands. We can see that the Bollinger band width indicator is dropping, again confirming that we are in a period of consolidation and that volatility is falling.

Prepare for the Breakout

We have confirmed that volatility is falling, but this doesn't give us an indication as to the direction of any potential breakout. This is because volatility has no directional bias; we don't know the direction of the next move, we know only that a move is imminent. Because of this, we need to prepare for a breakout in either direction.

We can do this by adding trend lines to the chart and targeting a break above or below a trend line as an entry point for a directional trade. If the upper trend line breaks, we will go long, and if the lower trend line breaks, we will sell short.

To guard against a false breakout, we will place a stop below the upper trend line in the case of a long trade, and above the lower trend line if we enter a short trade. Note that the two trend lines form a symmetrical triangle, a common formation during times of low volatility (see Figure ure 13.3).

Getting Out

Now that we have our entry points, we need to determine our exit points. When doing this, we want to consider price areas that have previously acted as support or resistance, as well as major Fibonacci retracements and round numbers.

For example, if the price breaks down past the lower trend line, initiating a short sale, the level of 1.2000 is an obvious choice for an exit. Although this area was briefly violated in early July, it had acted as strong support

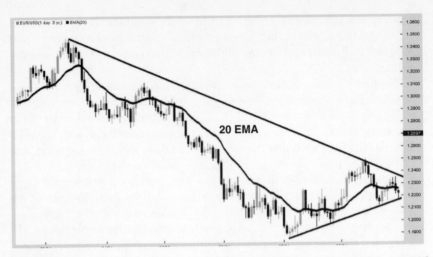

FIGURE 13.3 Trend lines form a symmetrical triangle, common during times of low volatility.

Source: FXtrek IntelliChart™. Copyright © 2001–2006 FXtrek.com, Inc.

on numerous occasions going back to the summer of 2004, and held firm on several occasions after its violation in late July 2005. It is also a round number, which can often create psychological support or resistance (see Figure 13.4).

A further level of possible support would be 1.1865, which at the time represented the lowest point reached by the pair since May 2004.

This second support level may prove useful if the trader decides to exit the position in increments; when the first exit is reached, the trader can exit half of the position and move the stop down to the breakeven point. This way, the trader can lock in a profit, eliminate any remaining risk by moving the stop to breakeven and give the remaining portion of the trade a chance to become a significant winner.

What if the price breaks the upper trend line, indicating that we should enter a long position? For resistance levels, we can draw a Fibonacci retracement of the major downward move from 1.3485 to 1.1865. The 38.2 percent retracement of this downtrend, located near 1.2485, made for a particularly compelling exit point because it had already held firm when it was tested August 11–12, 2005.

It is also in the vicinity of another large round number, 1.2500. Really, there are three good reasons to exit the trade when the price reaches the 1.2485/1.2500 area: a prior successful test of resistance, the 38.2-percent Fibonacci retracement level, and the large round number of 1.2500.

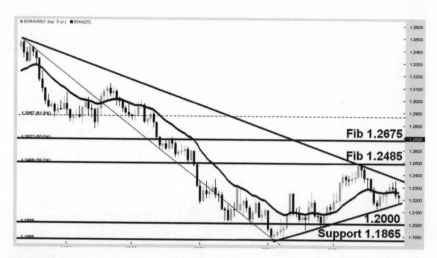

FIGURE 13.4 Exits are prepared for a breakout in either direction.

Source: FXtrek IntelliChart™. Copyright © 2001–2006 FXtrek.com, Inc.

A subsequent area of resistance would be 1.2675, the 50 percent Fibonacci retracement level of the same downtrend. Again, if we reach the first exit point, we can exit half of the position and raise the stop to the breakeven point on the remaining portion of the trade.

Longer Consolidation Equals Stronger Breakout

The longer the amount of time spent in the consolidation phase, the stronger the breakout tends to be. Why would this be true? Consider that during the time that the price is trading in a narrow range, there are buyers and sellers taking positions.

Because the price is not moving very much, these traders have little reason to exit their trades. But if the price breaks out in either direction, there are likely to be a large number of traders who are caught on the "wrong side" of the market, regardless of the direction of the breakout. As these traders cover their positions, they provide fuel for the breakout, helping to push the price further away from the consolidation area.

On Thursday, September 1, 2005, a weak U.S. economic report served as the catalyst as the euro/U.S. dollar (EUR/USD) pair blasted out of the area of consolidation and raced to the first target for long trades (see Figure 13.5). The currency pair reached a high of 1.2525 on the day of the breakout, as volatility returned with a vengeance—the 200-pip move was nearly double the average daily range.

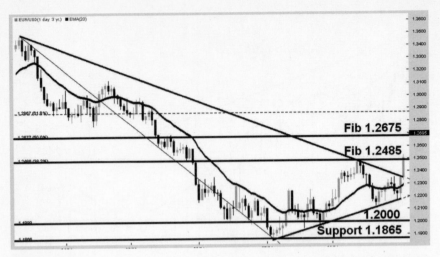

FIGURE 13.5 Volatility returns with a vengeance, as EUR/USD reaches its first target.

Source: FXtrek IntelliChart™. Copyright © 2001–2006 FXtrek.com, Inc.

Although this particular example occurs on the daily chart, similar setups also occur in other time frames. The logic behind the setup, and the forex market's tendency to break out after a period of consolidation, holds true in both long and short time frames.

VOLATILITY BREAKOUT STRATEGY

In this example, the Great Britain pound/U.S. dollar (GBP/USD) currency pair is in a strong downtrend in late 2005. By the spring of 2006, the pair had settled into a tight consolidation (see Figure 13.6).

As the pair transitions from high to low volatility, the 20-period EMA begins moving sideways. The flat 20-period EMA is one indication that the trend has paused, at least temporarily, and the price has entered the consolidation phase.

In order to confirm that a trade is setting up, the trader adds the ATR and Bollinger band width indicators to measure volatility. The ATR indicator is falling, meaning that the average daily range is shrinking. The Bollinger band width indicator has fallen to near its lows, again confirming that we are in a period of consolidation (see Figure 13.7).

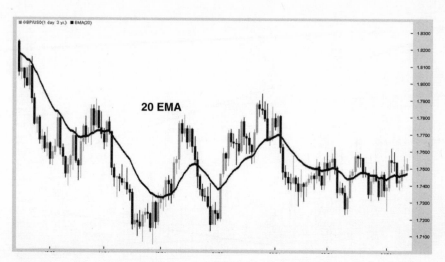

FIGURE 13.6 On the daily chart, GBP/USD consolidates after a volatile period.

Source: FXtrek IntelliChart™. Copyright © 2001–2006 FXtrek.com, Inc.

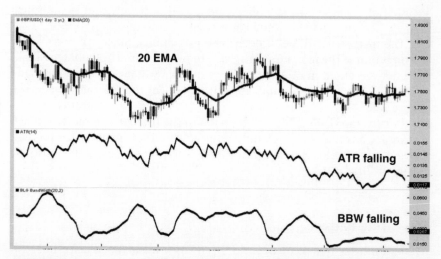

FIGURE 13.7 ATR and Bollinger band width indicate that volatility is falling.

Source: FXtrek IntelliChart™. Copyright © 2001–2006 FXtrek.com, Inc.

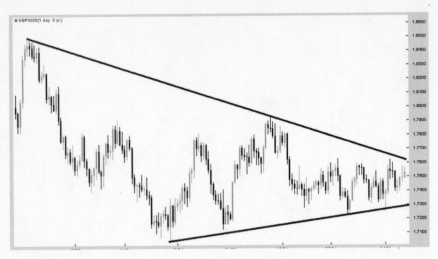

FIGURE 13.8   As volatility falls, a symmetrical triangle has formed in GBP/USD.

Source: FXtrek IntelliChart™. Copyright © 2001–2006 FXtrek.com, Inc.

Trend lines are then added to create entry points, and to determine the location of stops. As the trendlines are added to the chart, a symmetrical triangle becomes evident (see Figure 13.8).

The next step will be to determine exit points. Since we don't know the direction of the next move, we have to prepare for a potential breakout in either direction. In order to create exits, we will use prior support and resistance levels, round numbers, and Fibonacci retracement levels (see Figure 13.9).

Finally, the GBP/USD pair blasts out of the triangle and races to reach its targets, as once again volatility returns with a vengeance. This forceful move carried cable all the way to 1.9000, a move of nearly 1,500 pips (see Figure 13.10).

Repeating Pattern

Traders will see this setup occur over and over again (see Figure 13.11). It works so well because of the recurring cycle of volatility, which is made constant by human behavior. Markets may change over time and traders may come and go, but human nature remains basically the same. It is human nature that creates these market tendencies, and the trading techniques that recognize these tendencies will be useful for many years to come.

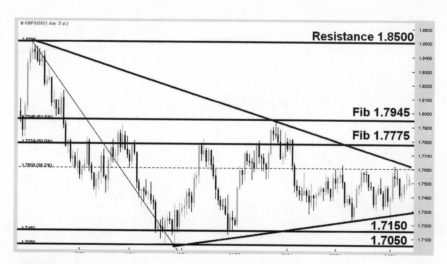

FIGURE 13.9 Use of support/resistance, round numbers and Fibonacci to determine exits.

Source: FXtrek IntelliChart™. Copyright © 2001–2006 FXtrek.com, Inc.

FIGURE 13.10 A huge breakout in GBP/USD carries the pair past its targets.

Source: FXtrek IntelliChart™. Copyright © 2001–2006 FXtrek.com, Inc.

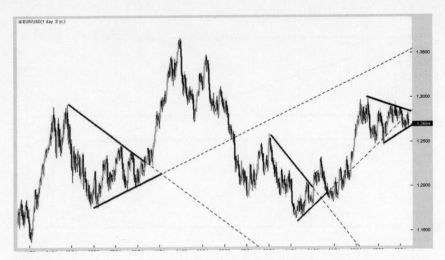

FIGURE 13.11   The cycle of volatility is evident in the EUR/USD currency pair.

Source: FXtrek IntelliChart™. Copyright © 2001–2006 FXtrek.com, Inc.

CHAPTER 14

The Round Trip

On a hot day, two friends are walking through the park. The temperature is exactly 94 degrees Fahrenheit, and the humidity is high. One casually remarks to the other, "It feels like 100 degrees out here!"

A child wants to go to the movies with her friends. She needs a precise total of $18.35 plus tax for a ticket, a beverage, and a snack. She asks her mother, "Mom, could I have $20 please?"

A woman and her husband are interested in buying beachfront property. The price of the house is listed at $2,095,000. The next day, they present an offer to buy the property for $2 million.

What do these seemingly unrelated events have in common? In each case, someone eschews a more precise figure in favor of a round number.

The truth is that we are all drawn to round numbers, or numbers ending in zero. Wall Street traders are extremely fond of zeros, especially the kind that appear at the end of their bonus checks. Round numbers also have a major role to play in trading.

WHY ROUND NUMBERS CAPTURE OUR ATTENTION

In March of 1999, the Dow Jones Industrial Average approached the 10,000 mark for the first time, with the index teasing investors for about two weeks before finally closing above 10,000. The event was greeted with much fanfare, because it was such an important milestone.

Or was it? More than seven years later, in September of 2006, the widely followed index was trading at around 11,000. Investors who went long at the peak of the Dow 10,000 frenzy had little to show for it, a gain of about 10 percent over the course of seven years. These same investors probably wished they had bought real estate instead, which greatly outperformed most equity markets during this time.

In retrospect, Dow 10,000 was just another number, yet news of it filled the front pages of newspapers and magazines, and financial news channels ran four-hour television specials touting the milestone. At the time, the entire market was fixated on the figure.

Why are we fascinated by so-called round numbers? Some scientists believe that humans created a "base-10" numeric system because we are born with 10 fingers and 10 toes. Because of this, we began to think in terms of factors of 10.

WHY ROUND NUMBERS ARE EFFECTIVE

Investors and traders have a strong tendency to place orders that coincide with round numbers. Perhaps at some point you've heard an analyst say, "I would recommend buying stock XYZ if it falls to $20," or "I would be a seller of stock XYZ at $40."

Imagine that many traders have placed buy orders for stock XYZ at $20 per share, because they believe the stock is a bargain at that price. If the price falls to $20, what will happen?

At that point, the stock will encounter a large pool of buy orders. When these orders are triggered, they can unleash a tremendous amount of buying power. When buyers outnumber or are more aggressive than sellers, the price rises.

Essentially, the buyers have created a support level at $20, because of the many orders that have accumulated at that level. Traders refer to this as *psychological support*, because it is not based on any prior price action.

Although we used an imaginary stock in this example, this phenomenon is very real and occurs in all forms of trading, especially in the forex market. Why are currencies, commodities, and stocks all subject to the round number phenomenon? Because the attraction to round numbers is a part of human nature, and therefore it can occur in any market traded by humans.

ROUND NUMBERS AND FOREX

The influence of round numbers in the forex market can be profound. For example, in Figure 14.1, we see the U.S. dollar/Canadian dollar (USD/CAD) currency pair in early 2005, finding support repeatedly at 1.2000.

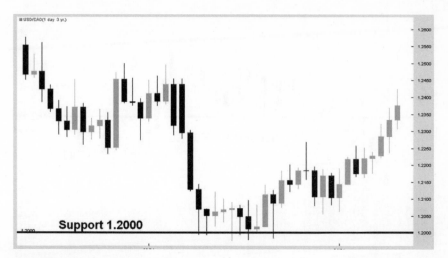

FIGURE 14.1 USD/CAD finds support repeatedly at a large round number (1.2000).

Source: FXtrek IntelliChart™. Copyright © 2001–2006 FXtrek.com, Inc.

In early 2006, euro/U.S. dollar (EUR/USD) buyers stepped in repeatedly in the vicinity of 1.2700 (see Figure 14.2). Traders who used these round numbers as entry points were rewarded handsomely. Let's look at a detailed method that we can use to benefit from this market tendency.

You might recall from an earlier strategy that a large pool of orders can create an attractive target, because banks earn commissions when their customers' orders are executed. Because orders tend to congregate at round numbers, we will take this tendency into consideration when creating our strategy.

THE FIRST BOUNCE IS THE BEST BOUNCE

The time frames will be unusually short for this day trading strategy. This is because the first bounce off of round number support or resistance is usually the best bounce, so we want to be certain that we are witnessing the first bounce. Longer time frames can hide multiple bounces within a single candle, so they cannot be used in this strategy.

Every time the exchange rate reaches the round number, orders are executed, and the pool of orders that creates the support or resistance level is diminished. Once the amount of orders remaining is no longer sufficient to repel the exchange rate, it's not unusual for the support or resistance level to eventually break.

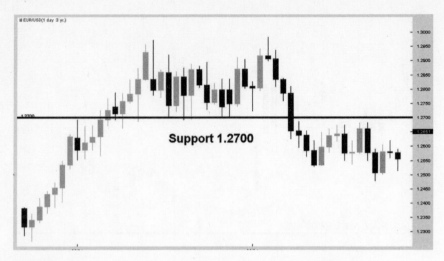

FIGURE 14.2 EUR/USD bounces repeatedly from the 1.2700 level.

Source: FXtrek IntelliChart™. Copyright © 2001–2006 FXtrek.com, Inc.

This is why it's important that we are trading the first bounce off of the round number, because it is at this point that the pool of orders is most effective. We can trade subsequent bounces as well, but the first bounce has the greatest potential.

USING THE MOVING AVERAGE

In order to be sure that we're not using a "stale" round number, the trade will be placed on a 5-, 10-, or 15-minute chart. In these time frames, a currency pair often tracks its 20-period moving average.

We're looking for a currency pair that suddenly "runs away" from its 20-period moving average. The pair should extend at least 20 pips away from the moving average. If it extends by more than 20 pips away from the moving average, that is not a problem; generally speaking, the further the extension, the better the trading opportunity.

The catalyst for this "extension" could be an economic indicator or other news event, but this is not a requirement. In this short-term trade, the reason behind the move is less important than the actual move itself.

If the currency pair is closing in on a potential cluster of orders at a round number, there is a chance that bank traders might try to give the exchange rate that little extra "push" needed to execute those orders. Once

FIGURE 14.3 USD/CAD races away from the 20-period moving average to the round number of 1.1400.

Source: FXtrek IntelliChart™. Copyright © 2001–2006 FXtrek.com, Inc.

the orders are executed, there is no reason for these traders to continue to pressure the exchange rate, and the pair often quickly reverses.

Here's an example; in Figure 14.3, the USD/CAD currency pair is tracking along its 20-period moving average on the 5-minute chart (see Figure 14.3). Suddenly, the pair races away from the 20-period moving average toward the round number of 1.1400. The exchange rate touches the figure, causing any orders located at 1.1400 to be executed, and then fades back to the 20-period moving average.

If the pair is extended away from the 20-period moving average by at least 20 pips, we will enter a trade in the vicinity of the round number. As the exchange rate is climbing higher, we will sell short at the figure, and if it is moving lower, we will go long at the round number.

Placing the Stop

The protective stop will be 15 pips, *plus the spread*, from the entry point. So, if you were trading a pair that has a spread of 3 pips, then your stop would be 18 pips away from your entry point. If the pair had a 4-pip spread, the stop would be 19 pips away.

You would never, under any circumstances, enter a trade using this strategy with a currency pair that has a spread of more than 5 pips. This is because the spread has a greater impact on short-term trades than it does on trades with a longer time horizon. Using a pair with a wide spread will reduce your chances of success, because intraday trades take place on a smaller "playing field," where every pip takes on added significance.

THE STRATEGY IN ACTION

Now that we understand the overall concept, let's take a detailed look at a series of trades that were placed using this technique. First, the USD/CAD exchange rate begins to move away from the 20-period simple moving average (SMA). At this point it is not yet extended by the minimum requirement of 20 pips, but the situation bears watching. The trader prepares for a potential entry opportunity (see Figure 14.4).

The pair continues to run toward the figure of 1.1400. By the time it reaches this point, the pair is extended more than 20 pips above the 20-period SMA. The trader enters a short position, in the vicinity of 1.1400 (see Figure 14.5).

In this case the pair has a spread of 4 pips, so our stop is located at 1.1419 (15 pips, plus the 4-pip spread, above the entry point). Remember; *never* attempt to use this technique when the currency pair has a spread of more than 5 pips.

Now we need to create our exits. Just as we did in one of the earlier trend following strategies, we will take a partial exit when the pair moves in our favor by an amount equivalent to the amount at risk. Since our risk

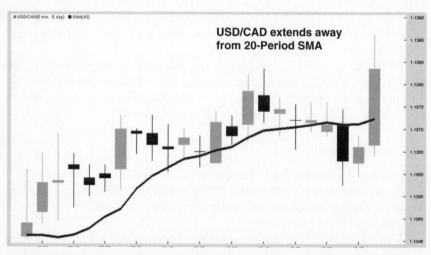

FIGURE 14.4 USD/CAD exchange rate extends away from the 20-period SMA.

Source: FXtrek IntelliChart™. Copyright © 2001–2006 FXtrek.com, Inc.

FIGURE 14.5 Short selling opportunity in USD/CAD at 1.1400.

Source: FXtrek IntelliChart™. Copyright © 2001–2006 FXtrek.com, Inc.

equals 19 pips per lot, we will exit half of the position when we are profitable by 19 pips.

In this case, the first exit would be 1.1381 (the entry point of 1.1400 minus 19 pips). This will lock in a small profit, while allowing for a larger potential gain.

At the same time that we take our partial exit, we will lower the stop to our entry point of 1.1400 (see Figure 14.6). This eliminates any further risk from the trade and gives us a worst-case scenario of a profitable trade.

You'll notice that 19 pips is a pretty small profit compared to some of our earlier examples. At this point, I'm often asked why I don't let that initial profit run further. The answer is that this is designed to be a short-term trade, just a quick reaction to a sudden move toward a pool of orders.

To try to bend this strategy into something it's not would be unadvisable. Every strategy is designed to capitalize on a market tendency, and the moves that occur in reaction to round numbers tend to be swift and brief. It is not a long-term setup, and it shouldn't be treated as such.

Also, you'll notice that in Figure 14.6 the exchange rate has snapped right back to the 20-period SMA. Does that mean that the 20-period SMA is a good exit point? Not necessarily. There are too many variables regarding the 20-period SMA to use it as a part of the exit strategy.

For example, in this case, when we entered the trade, the exchange rate was extended away from the moving average by a little more than

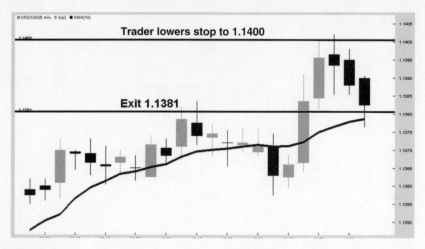

FIGURE 14.6 The first exit is reached, and the stop is lowered to the breakeven point.

Source: FXtrek IntelliChart™. Copyright © 2001–2006 FXtrek.com, Inc.

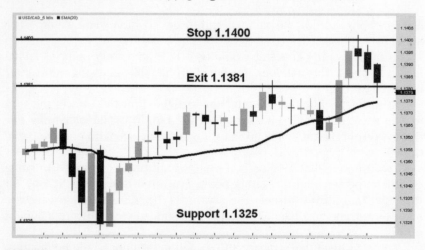

FIGURE 14.7 Prior support is located near 1.1325, our second exit.

Source: FXtrek IntelliChart™. Copyright © 2001–2006 FXtrek.com, Inc.

20 pips. What if it were extended by 60 pips? Using the 20-period SMA to determine our exit would create a very different exit from our original scenario.

Instead, my preferred method for exiting the remainder of the position would be to search for prior support levels. Remember, price is the ultimate indicator. In Figure 14.7, we can see that after a recent selloff, the exchange

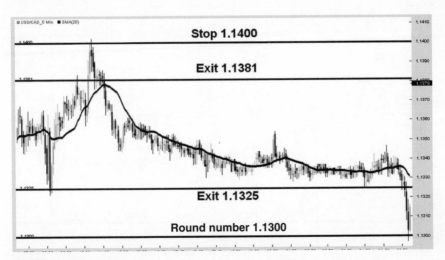

FIGURE 14.8 As the first USD/CAD trade ends, a long entry is created at 1.1300.

Source: FXtrek IntelliChart™. Copyright © 2001–2006 FXtrek.com, Inc.

rate bounced sharply from the area near 1.1325, so we will use this level as our next exit.

By the next day, the exit of 1.1325 has been reached, for a gain of 75 pips. Notice how the exchange rate continues to fall past our exit of 1.1325, all the way down to—you guessed it—the round number of 1.1300.

The quick plunge to the round number causes the price to extend away from the 20-period SMA by more than 20 pips. This creates another trade setup based on the same principles that we just discussed, except this time we will be trading from the long side (see Figure 14.8).

The round number of 1.1300 will be our entry point for a long trade. You might recall that in our first trade, our stop was 19 pips above the entry point. We will use the same equation here (15 pips plus the spread of 4 pips) to create our stop of 19 pips. Since this is a long trade, the stop will be 19 pips *below* our entry point. This gives our stop an initial location of 1.1281 (see Figure 14.9).

This time, the exchange rate will give us a scare as it slides beneath 1.1300 and approaches our stop at 1.1281. Luckily, the pair bottoms out at 1.1290 before turning to move higher.

We will exit a portion of the trade when the profit is equal to the risk. Since our risk on the trade is equal to 19 pips per lot, our first exit will be located at 1.1319 (entry point of 1.1300 plus the risk of 19 pips). At the same time that we take our partial profit, we'll move our stop up to the break-even point of 1.1300 (see Figure 14.10).

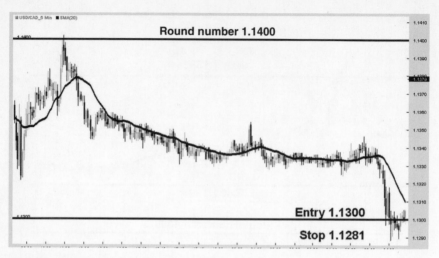

FIGURE 14.9 The initial stop is located at 1.1281.

Source: FXtrek IntelliChart™. Copyright © 2001–2006 FXtrek.com, Inc.

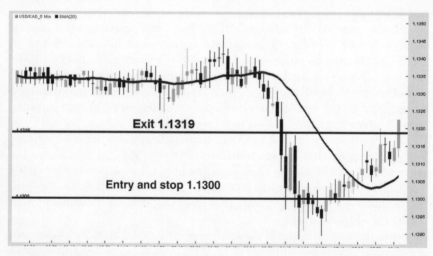

FIGURE 14.10 As the first exit is reached, the stop is raised to the entry point (breakeven).

Source: FXtrek IntelliChart™. Copyright © 2001–2006 FXtrek.com, Inc.

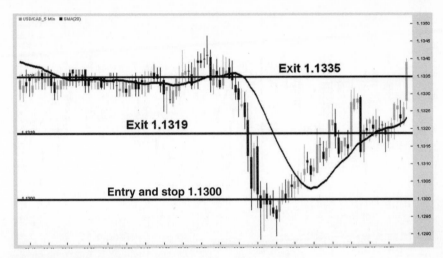

FIGURE 14.11 The second exit is reached at 1.1335.

Source: FXtrek IntelliChart™. Copyright © 2001–2006 FXtrek.com, Inc.

We still need to determine our secondary exit. There is a clear area of resistance visible in Figure 14.11, a horizontal band that ranges from about 1.1330 to 1.1340. Although this represents a less ambitious gain than the one from our prior trade, the resistance level dictates our exit point. We'll place our exit right in the middle of that band of resistance, at 1.1335. A few hours later, the exchange rate reaches our exit for a profit of 35 pips.

After our exit is achieved, the price drops again and finds support once again—at the round number of 1.1300 (see Figure 14.12). The entire sequence is set into motion once again, with the same entry, stop, and exit points.

Remember, while we prefer to trade the first bounce, we can enter a trade on a subsequent bounce off of the round number. Just be aware that with each subsequent test, the pool of orders is diminished and the chances for a successful trade are decreased.

This "ping-pong effect" can occur because, in addition to the round number, there is now prior price support that was created by the earlier bounce off of the figure. An observant trader can catch a series of good trades in this fashion.

It's worth noting that some currency pairs seem to be more sensitive to the round number phenomenon than others. This does not limit the strategy in any way, as round numbers can impact any currency pair at any time. For instance, round numbers come into play quite often in the USD/CAD and Great Britain pound/U.S. dollar (GBP/USD) pairs.

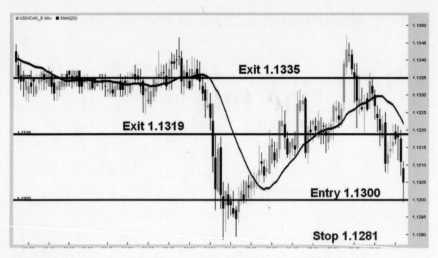

FIGURE 14.12 The USD/CAD exchange rate falls to 1.1300 again, creating another entry.

Source: FXtrek IntelliChart™. Copyright © 2001–2006 FXtrek.com, Inc.

I am not aware of any logical explanation for why these particular currency pairs are more inclined to find support or resistance at a round number than other pairs; it's just something that I've observed over time.

I've also seen round number support/resistance occur frequently in some of the Yen pairs, particularly euro/Japanese yen (EUR/JPY) and USD/JPY. On those pairs, the midway point between round numbers (for example 114.50, or 137.50) can also act as support or resistance. Could a trader adapt this strategy to incorporate these semi-round numbers? Perhaps, but your chances for success will be greater if you stick with the true round numbers—ones that end in two or more zeroes.

CHAPTER 15

The Interest Rate Edge

Wouldn't it be nice to get something for nothing? Wouldn't it be great if the next time you filled up your tank, the station attendant gave you a few extra gallons of gas (or liters of petrol, for my friends outside the United States) at no cost?

Or how about if you went to dinner, and after a sumptuous meal, the maître d' refused to accept payment. "This one's on us," she says. "Please come again soon!"

Sounds too good to be true, doesn't it? That's because we've been conditioned to believe that if something sounds too good to be true, it often is. In the real world, there is always a hidden "catch." But occasionally, there really is a way to "beat the system."

For instance, wouldn't it be great if the next time you entered a forex trade, you turned a profit even though the currency pair didn't budge? Wouldn't it be nice to make money off of your trades, even when the market is uncooperative? Do you think this would make trading easier?

If you answered yes, you'd be correct. Although it may sound far-fetched to the uninitiated, this is exactly how the "big boys"—banks, hedge funds, and other institutional traders—play the forex game.

THINK LIKE THE BIG BOYS

This technique requires that we think big, in terms of both potential profit and time. The long-term forex trader's perspective is similar to that of the institutional trader, because hedge funds and institutions tend to hold foreign exchange trades for months at a time.

Since institutional money is the so-called "smart money," we can learn from their techniques and adapt them to our own trading. The individual long-term forex trader can use the same techniques, and garner the same benefits, that hedge funds and institutions have enjoyed for years.

INTEREST RATE DIFFERENTIALS

The heart of this technique lies in interest rate arbitrage, and in the fact that every currency has a corresponding rate of interest. This rate is determined by the central bank of the nation or nations that use the currency. For example, the Federal Reserve sets U.S. interest rates, while the European Central Bank determines the interest rate for Germany, France, and the other nations of the European Monetary Union.

Since currencies trade in pairs, and each currency has a corresponding interest rate, then within every currency pair there are two different rates of interest. Usually, there is some disparity between the rates, so in almost every case, one currency has a higher yield than the other member of the pair.

Here is the edge that the big institutional traders seek to exploit; in every forex trade, the trader is long one currency and short one currency. The trader who is long the higher yielding of the two currencies collects interest on the trade.

Conversely, the trader who is short the higher yielding of the two currencies must pay interest. The amount of interest that the trader either collects or pays is based on the interest rate differential, which is simply the difference in interest rates between the two currencies.

HERE'S HOW IT WORKS

Assume that a trade is placed in the fictional currency pair ABC/XYZ. The interest rate for currency ABC is 4.0 percent, while the rate for currency XYZ is 1.0 percent.

Therefore, ABC is the higher yielding of the two currencies. Traders who are long ABC and short XYZ will collect 3.0 percent interest, which is the differential between ABC and XYZ (4.0 percent − 1.0 percent = 3.0 percent). Remember, you must be long the higher-yielding currency to collect interest.

Conversely, traders who are long XYZ and short ABC must pay that same 3.0 percent interest rate differential. Arbitrage traders who are long the higher-yielding currency seek to collect interest every day, for as long as they hold the currency pair.

I know this seems simple, but there is much more to this strategy than simply matching up a high-yielding currency against a low-yielding currency. Ideally, traders use this strategy when they can identify a situation where the interest rate differential is likely to expand over time.

This would result in an even greater payoff for the trader who is long the higher-yielding currency. Traders exit the strategy when it becomes apparent that the differential will stop growing or become smaller in the future.

CHANGING DIFFERENTIALS

Let's revisit the previous example. Assume again that we are trading currency pair ABC/XYZ, and we are collecting interest because we are long currency ABC and short currency XYZ.

If the economy of ABC is strong, ABC's central bank is likely to raise interest rates to contain growth and control inflation. When the central bank takes action, ABC's interest rate rises from 4.0 percent to 4.25 percent, causing the differential to widen from 3.0 percent to 3.25 percent (4.25 percent − 1.0 percent = 3.25 percent).

Similarly, if the economy of currency XYZ is weak, then XYZ's central bank is likely to lower interest rates to spur demand and promote growth. XYZ's interest rate is lowered from 1.0 percent to 0.75 percent, and the differential has now grown to 3.5 percent (4.25 percent − 0.75 percent = 3.5 percent).

Traders, encouraged by the growing interest rate differential, go long ABC and sell short XYZ, in order to collect the additional interest. If enough traders can be enticed to go long ABC and sell short XYZ, this will create positive pressure on ABC and negative pressure on XYZ. Consequently, the ABC/XYZ currency pair begins to rise.

This creates a kind of "chicken-and-egg" scenario; is the pair rising because traders are entering to collect the interest, or is the relative strength and weakness of the two economies causing the pair to rally, with the bulging interest differential as a mere side effect?

In truth, both of these explanations could be considered accurate, as they are not mutually exclusive. Traders who are long the ABC/XYZ pair are experiencing the best of both worlds, as they are now benefiting from exchange rate appreciation and the interest rate differential.

WHAT'S THE BIG DEAL?

At this point, readers may be wondering why traders would be excited about collecting an interest rate differential of 3.0 percent or 3.5 percent. While the amount of interest may not seem significant at first glance, a closer look will reveal the secret as to why hedge funds and institutions favor this strategy.

In reference to a trader collecting 3.5 percent interest on the trade, the 3.5 percent is based on a nonleveraged transaction. For instance, if a trader is long one lot of the U.S. dollar/Japanese yen (USD/JPY) currency pair, he or she is long approximately 100,000 U.S. dollars and short an equivalent amount of Japanese Yen.

If we assume an interest rate differential of 3.5 percent, this means that over the course of a year, the trader would collect approximately 3.5 percent of $100,000, or about $3,500, if he or she is long the higher-yielding currency (USD).

Here's the good part: Due to the tremendous leverage afforded by the forex market, traders do not have to put up 100 percent of the value of a currency pair in order to control that investment. For example, a trader using leverage of 50–1 would need to invest only $2,000 to control one lot of a currency pair, instead of the full amount of $100,000.

The trader is not penalized for using leverage, and collects the full 3.5 percent interest on the entire $100,000 ($3,500), even though the trader only had to invest a fraction of that amount ($2,000).

This creates a much higher return on investment, and helps to explain the popularity of this technique. It is also important to note that leverage is a "double-edged sword," which can lead to rapid losses as well as rapid gains.

COLLECTING INTEREST

The advantage of this technique from the trader's perspective is that he or she might turn a profit regardless of whether the trade moves in the desired direction. For example, if the trade remains flat for months, the trader could still come out ahead as long as he or she collects interest. This provides a tremendous edge.

Compare this situation to that of the person who is on the opposite side of the trade; he or she must pay interest every day, regardless of whether the trade moves in the desired direction. The trader who is short the higher-yielding currency must regain the lost interest in order to break even.

An informative example of the effect that swings in interest rates can have on currencies can be seen in the USD/JPY currency pair. In order to fight deflation, Japan kept interest rates near zero percent for several years. This extraordinarily low interest rate made the yen a popular currency to sell short in the forex carry trade.

Japan's central bank, the Bank of Japan, eventually raised interest rates and put an end to this zero-interest-rate policy. However, throughout the span of time covered in the following example, Japan's interest rate was virtually zero percent.

U.S. DOLLAR/JAPANESE YEN

During the years 2002 through 2004, the U.S. dollar was in a persistent downtrend versus the Japanese yen (see Figure 15.1). After experiencing outstanding growth in the late 1990s, the U.S. economy had faltered.

In order to stimulate growth, the U.S. Federal Reserve, under the leadership of Alan Greenspan, reduced the benchmark U.S. overnight lending rate to near-historic lows, and U.S. rates bottomed out at 1.0 percent in mid-2003.

With the interest rate differential between the U.S. dollar and the Japanese yen at 1.0 percent, and the U.S. economy in a tailspin, traders had little incentive to go long the currency pair. The USD/JPY exchange

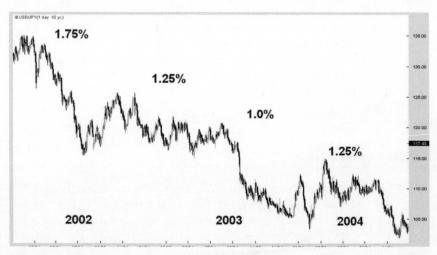

FIGURE 15.1 U.S. dollar falls versus yen as the interest rate differential narrows.

Source: FXtrek IntelliChart™. Copyright © 2001–2006 FXtrek.com, Inc.

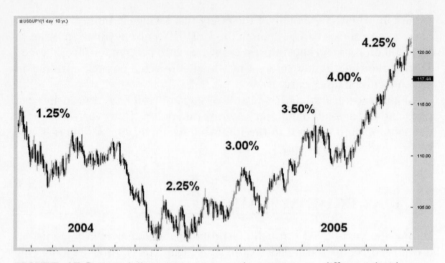

FIGURE 15.2   U.S. dollar gains vs. yen as the interest rate differential widens.

Source: FXtrek IntelliChart™. Copyright © 2001–2006 FXtrek.com, Inc.

rate responded by plunging over 3,000 pips, falling from over 135 yen per U.S. dollar in early 2002, down to less than 105 yen per U.S. dollar by late 2004.

The Federal Reserve's prolonged low-interest-rate policy, combined with tax cuts, gradually stimulated growth in the U.S. economy. By the middle of 2004, the Federal Reserve began to reverse its policy, with the first of what would become a series of interest rate increases.

The U.S. central bank felt it was necessary to gradually remove economic stimulation, in an effort to keep growth and inflation at manageable levels. For the first time in years, the interest rate differential between the U.S. dollar and the Japanese yen began to widen (see Figure 15.2).

LONG-TERM PLAY

The Federal Reserve continued to raise interest rates throughout 2005, while the Bank of Japan maintained its zero interest rate policy. As the interest rate differential widened, traders increasingly favored long positions in the USD/JPY currency pair, in order to both capture the yield and to benefit from the U.S. economic recovery.

As more traders entered and expanded their long positions, the pair began a spectacular climb that lasted throughout most of the year 2005.

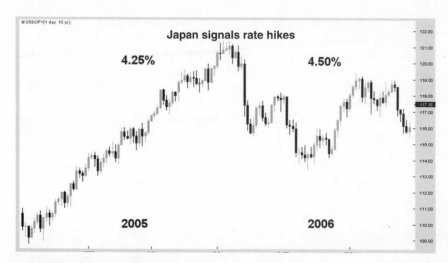

FIGURE 15.3 Uptrend dissolves as U.S. and Japan central banks signal policy changes.

Source: FXtrek IntelliChart™. Copyright © 2001–2006 FXtrek.com, Inc.

Traders enjoyed the dual benefits of interest and appreciation, as the pair climbed nearly 2,000 pips during the year.

By late 2005, the interest rate differential on the USD/JPY currency pair had widened to 4.25 percent, yet the pair experienced a sharp sell-off. The differential continued to increase early in 2006, yet the pair lost traction, and the once ferocious upward trend dissolved into a trading range (see Figure 15.3).

LOOKING AHEAD

At first glance, the sell off in U.S. dollar/Japanese yen seems to contradict the swelling interest rate differential, but only if we forget that financial markets are forward looking.

Near the end of 2005, the U.S. Federal Reserve, while still raising interest rates, signaled that changes in monetary policy would be forthcoming, and that the long series of U.S. rate hikes was coming to an end. The interest rate differential between the U.S. dollar and the Japanese yen was about to reach its peak.

Around that same time, amid signs that deflation was under control, the Bank of Japan indicated that the days of its ultra-easy monetary policy would soon be over. The differential was about to narrow; arbitrage traders quickly headed for the exits, closing out positions in what for some had become a phenomenally successful trade.

Traders who attempt to take advantage of interest rate differentials have a long-term outlook, and intend to stay in their trades for months at a time. As a result, this causes these traders to have a very forward-looking focus on the forex markets.

Traders are not going to wait for an actual policy change to occur before taking action. Instead, like master chess players, they plan their moves well in advance. For these traders, the comments from the respective central banks hinting at changes in monetary policy were the proverbial writing on the wall. The time had come to take profits and move on, in search of the next great forex trading opportunity.

CHAPTER 16

The Boomerang

S o far, we have discussed a variety of strategies, each based on some tendency of the forex market. There is another tendency that we haven't yet discussed—the tendency of the forex market to be very quiet at certain times of the trading day.

There is a stretch of several hours, starting after the U.S. forex session ends and prior to the beginning of the Asian session, which tends to be very low in volume. Although the Australian and New Zealand forex markets are active at this time of day, the overall volume is relatively slight.

This is because the "big three" of forex trading (Great Britain, the United States, and Japan) are mostly inactive at this time of day. Under these conditions, currency pairs tend to drift, and any movement in the market becomes highly suspect.

FADING FALSE BREAKOUTS

Breakouts that occur during these hours are notoriously unreliable, because they almost always occur on very low volume. A trending technique would be inappropriate during these hours due to the overall lack of market direction. Since any movement that occurs at this time is unreliable and likely to retrace, we can create a strategy that is designed to capitalize on these false breakouts, by "fading" or trading against them.

Since this time of day is also considered to be the beginning of the forex trading day, it is also the same time that many (but not all) market makers choose to charge or credit interest. However, unlike an interest rate arbitrage strategy, this short-term trade is not designed to collect interest.

We will incorporate a defense against interest rate charges by entering our orders just after 17:00 Eastern (New York) time. This will equate to 22:00 GMT during standard hours, or 21:00 GMT during Daylight Saving Time, also known as "Summer Hours." Either way, the time of day for this trade will always be just after 17:00 Eastern U.S. time.

THE STRATEGY

This strategy is specifically designed for the euro/U.S. dollar (EUR/USD) currency pair. The plan is to enter a sell order above the market, in order to fade a move higher, and at the same time enter a buy order beneath the market, to trade against a move lower. In both cases we are assuming that any directional movement is false, and the exchange rate is likely to retrace.

Such a directional move is likely to be caused by a large order, which would not have the power to move the market under normal circumstances. Since the volume is extremely low at this time of day, these orders now have the ability to create market movement under "thin" trading conditions.

SETTING THE PARAMETERS

The sell order will be located 15 pips above the "opening" price, and the buy order 15 pips below. Our stops will be located 15 pips away, creating a risk/reward ratio of 1:1 for the trade (one pip of risk per one pip of potential reward).

Since this trade is only designed for only one currency pair, the EUR/USD pair, we can set fixed-pip parameters. If this technique were attempted with any other currency pair, the parameters would have to be adjusted to account for the difference in volatility.

The trader would also have to consider that the spread for most currency pairs is wider than EUR/USD. Because the "playing field" for this trade will be small, every pip takes on added importance.

This is a brief, "slingshot"-style trade that is designed for quick profits, perfect for EUR/USD. This pair tends to have a very narrow spread, making it ideal for a short-term trade.

ENTERING THE TRADE

Let's take a look at this concept in action. At 17:00 Eastern U.S. time, the opening price on the five-minute EUR/USD chart is 1.2583 (see Figure 16.1). We'll place a sell order 15 pips above the opening price at 1.2598, and a buy order 15 pips below the open at 1.2568.

If we do not have a trade execution within two hours, we will cancel both the buy and sell orders. At that point, the reason for placing the trade is no longer valid, because the Asian markets are beginning to stir, and volume and volatility are about to increase. When real volume enters the market, the moves are more likely to be real, so a strategy that fades breakouts would be inappropriate under these circumstances.

After initially drifting higher, the exchange rate drops, and the buy order is executed at 1.2568 (see Figure 16.2). Our stop is located 15 pips below the entry point, at 1.2553. This is very important—we immediately cancel the sell order at 1.2598. Our target will be a modest return to the opening price, or 1.2583.

Within a few hours, the exchange rate aimlessly drifts toward the exit point of 1.2583, and the trade is completed (see Figure 16.3). The trader has the option of exiting the entire position, or closing a portion of the trade and moving the stop to the breakeven point.

FIGURE 16.1 The EUR/USD "opens" at 1.2583; the buy order is executed at 1.2568.

Source: FXtrek IntelliChart(tm). Copyright © 2001–2006 FXtrek.com, Inc.

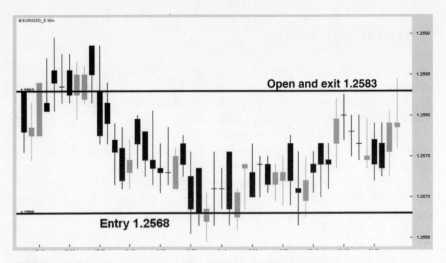

FIGURE 16.2   The entry point of 1.2583 is also the exit point.

Source: FXtrek IntelliChart(tm). Copyright © 2001–2006 FXtrek.com, Inc.

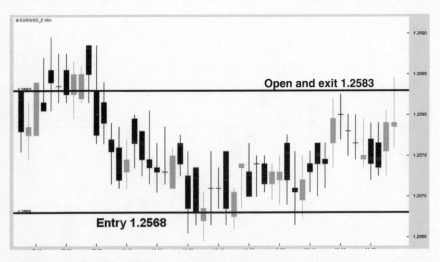

FIGURE 16.3   The exchange rate reaches the exit point of 1.2583.

Source: FXtrek IntelliChart(tm). Copyright © 2001–2006 FXtrek.com, Inc.

SIMPLE BUT EFFECTIVE

This method is simple, but it's also effective because the exchange rate rarely makes a big move during this "dead zone" between the U.S. and Asian sessions.

In order for the stop to be reached, the exchange rate for the EUR/USD would have to move 30 pips in one direction—15 pips to trigger the entry, and another 15 pips to reach the stop—a rarity at this time of the trading day.

Here's another example: At 17:00 Eastern U.S. time, the exchange rate shows an opening price of 1.2636 (see Figure 16.4). The trader places a sell order 15 pips above at 1.2651, and a buy order 15 pips below at 1.2621. The buy order is executed at 1.2621, and we immediately cancel the sell order at 1.2651.

The stop is located 15 pips below our entry point, at 1.2606. After the execution, the exchange rate drifts higher, and returns to the opening price of 1.2636, which also serves as our exit.

This tactic is a nice addition to your arsenal of trading techniques; it is intended for those "quiet times" when trading opportunities are rare. The intention is to get in and get out quickly. While the gains are not large, the percentage of winners should be high, because of the market's tendency to drift at this time of day.

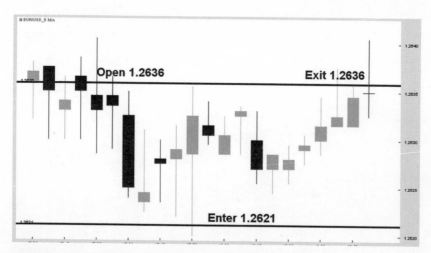

FIGURE 16.4 EUR/USD dips to provide an entry, and then reverses toward the exit point.

Source: FXtrek IntelliChart(tm). Copyright © 2001–2006 FXtrek.com, Inc.

Here is one more important point to consider: This strategy assumes that interest will be charged or credited at a particular time of day. While many market makers charge or credit interest at 17:00 Eastern U.S. time, this is not a uniform practice. Rules for the payment or collection of interest vary from one market maker to the next, so be sure to check with your broker for these important details before attempting to place a trade using this strategy.

PART IV

Take Control of Your Trading Destiny

There is more to trading than just techniques and patterns. There are many obstacles on the path to success. Only by truly understanding the trading environment—and ourselves—do we have a chance to achieve our full potential.

CHAPTER 17

How to Achieve Spectacular Gains

When I was 14 years old, I spent my life savings of $100 on a beat-up used guitar and an amplifier. After a few years of daily practice, I learned how to play lead guitar proficiently, and by the age of 17 I made my debut as a professional musician.

I love rock music, and as the years passed I took great pleasure in learning how to perform some of the most difficult and inspiring classic rock guitar solos. I emulated players like Jimi Hendrix, Randy Rhoads, Jimmy Page, Ritchie Blackmore, Brian May, and Joe Satriani—guitarists who were technically proficient, but also able to express a wide range of emotions musically and paint a vivid aural landscape. Later, I began to write songs and express myself through my own words and music.

Because of my involvement with music, I made a lot of friends and met many truly amazing people. Thanks to music, I've traveled extensively, dated beautiful women—in general, I've been treated like a rock star. I've heard the sound of my name being chanted by hundreds of people at once. My experiences in the music business are cherished and irreplaceable. I still play guitar today, and it's a big part of who I am.

All in all, not bad for a $100 initial investment. That's what I call a spectacular return!

Mind you, I didn't pick up the guitar and start playing the solo from "Stairway to Heaven" on the first day. No, this was a long, gradual process of achieving one plateau and then striving for the next one. I started with an easily achievable goal, to play a simple three-chord progression. I sounded horrible for the entire first year, but after a while, it all began to make sense, and the pieces of the musical puzzle began to fall into place. I made my way to the next plateau, and then the next, until I found myself playing professionally in front of a live audience.

In a way, playing guitar is a lot like trading. I'm going to show you how to achieve one plateau and then strive for the next one. Along the way, you'll gain knowledge, experience, and confidence, and the pieces of the trading puzzle will fall into place. Maybe trading will become a big part of who you are.

KEEP YOUR EYES ON THE ROAD

Around the same time that I was learning to play the guitar, I was also learning how to drive a car. I'll never forget my first few times behind the wheel—I could barely keep my Dad's Ford on the road! Just like many teenage drivers, I was a hazard on wheels until I gained a little experience. I was a prime candidate for an accident.

If you're new to trading, or even if you're an experienced but undisciplined trader, you are just like that teenage driver. You don't yet have the experience that allows good drivers—and good traders—to anticipate and avoid trouble. You are a prime candidate to do serious damage to your account.

Our goals must be in sync with where we stand as drivers or as traders. The teenage driver with a learner's permit should not have a goal of winning the Daytona 500; he or she should just concentrate on driving the car around the block without hitting anything.

Similarly, the newbie trader should not have a goal of doubling his or her account overnight. He or she should just concentrate on not blowing up the account.

Are spectacular gains possible? Absolutely, but don't expect everything to fall into place overnight. Just like the guitarist or the driver, we'll start with an easily achievable goal, and once we've conquered that first plateau, we'll move on to the next one, and then the next.

PROPER GOAL SETTING

It's understandable that traders sometimes get excited and "shoot for the moon" when they first get involved with trading. After all, a successful trading career presents us with the opportunity for an unparalleled lifestyle, short work hours, and most important of all, freedom—the freedom to be your own boss, to set your own schedule, to travel to faraway places and stay there for as long as you wish. I'm sure that we would all like at least a little bit more freedom in our lives and more control over our own destiny.

Because the prizes are so fantastic, it's easy to get excited and lose objectivity regarding trading. Excitement is an emotion that clouds our judgment, and often leads to unrealistic expectations. Trading requires that we keep ourselves free of emotion, so that we can make clear, rational decisions. This can be difficult when you're dreaming of owning a large beach house or a Gulfstream jet.

Traders who are trying to change their lives overnight often do so, but usually not for the better. Many traders enter this game with high expectations and are quickly vanquished. Remember that more traders fail than succeed, and the failure rate is especially high among new traders. What is needed is a commonsense method for setting goals.

The first thing we must do is to rid ourselves of unrealistic expectations; often, we obtain these expectations from things we have seen, read, or heard. For example, perhaps you've heard stories from a friend who bragged about making some outrageous amount of money, and you've decided that if he can do it, so can you.

I think that what you will find over time is that the truly good traders rarely talk about their gains; they know that the market has a way of humbling traders who get "carried away" or form too high of an opinion of themselves or their trading.

There are many traders who appear on the scene and immediately achieve great returns, only to give that money back to the market later. Anyone can make money in the market over a short period of time with a little luck, but this is most likely because they are probably using methods that have a high probability of short-term success but a very low probability of long-term success.

These new traders haven't learned the difference between a good trade and a winning trade; a good trade isn't always a winning trade, and a winning trade isn't always a good trade.

Instead of setting your sights too high, create goals that are attainable. The seeming contradiction here is that you can achieve some lofty goals if you're willing to break those goals into smaller pieces. So, instead of asking, "How much time will it take to double my account" (which is well within the realm of possibility if you are using methods that are geared toward long-term success), why not break that goal into smaller pieces?

The good thing about taking this approach is that you don't have to take crazy chances with your account to meet your goals and reap substantial gains. Traders are much more likely to violate their risk management rules when trying to achieve an unrealistic goal.

BREAKING DOWN YOUR GOALS

The way to achieve great results is to take an ambitious goal and break it down into small, achievable pieces.

When I give a seminar or address a group of traders, I sometimes ask the following question: "How many people in the room feel that a goal of a 100 percent annual return is an aggressive goal?" Many people in the room will raise their hands at this point, because a 100 percent annual return does seem to be an ambitious target.

Then, I'll follow up with this question: "How many people in the room feel that a goal of a *consistent* 6 percent monthly return is too aggressive?" The hands go down, as almost nobody in the room feels that this is an aggressive target.

The punch line is that the goals are one and the same. If a trader can increase the value of the account by just 6 percent per month on a consistent basis, he or she will achieve an annual gain of about 100 percent.

I know what some of you are thinking. "Wait a minute—6 percent per month multiplied by 12 months per year equals a 72 percent return, not a 100 percent return! Ed has surely lost his mind—from all that loud music, no doubt!"

Perhaps, but don't fit me for a straitjacket just yet. Whip out a calculator and perform the following exercise: Starting with a base number of 100 (the "account"), multiply by 1.06 (a 6 percent gain) to calculate your first month's result (106). Then multiply *that* result by 1.06, and keep doing this until you have calculated an entire year's worth of results (12 months). You should end up with the following (*note that some numbers are rounded, but this has no material effect on the results*):

Month 1: $100 \times 1.06 = 106.00$
Month 2: $106 \times 1.06 = 112.36$
Month 3: $112.36 \times 1.06 = 119.102$
Month 4: $119.102 \times 1.06 = 126.248$
Month 5: $126.248 \times 1.06 = 133.822$
Month 6: $133.822 \times 1.06 = 141.852$
Month 7: $141.852 \times 1.06 = 150.363$
Month 8: $150.363 \times 1.06 = 159.385$
Month 9: $159.385 \times 1.06 = 168.948$
Month 10: $168.948 \times 1.06 = 179.084$
Month 11: $179.084 \times 1.06 = 189.830$
Month 12: $189.830 \times 1.06 = 201.219$

The account has climbed from a base of 100 to over 200 in one year, an annual gain of just over 100 percent. In order to replicate the results for different-sized trading accounts, add zeros to the base as necessary. In other words, if the base were 1,000, or 10,000, or 100,000, the percentage gains would remain the same. Because the gains are a *consistent* 6 percent, we are building off of a higher base every month. This is similar to the power of compounding.

CONSISTENCY IS THE KEY

This is not to suggest that a monthly gain of 6 percent is easy to achieve, but it does demonstrate the power of breaking our goals down into manageable targets. Consistency is the key; it is not that difficult to achieve a 6 percent return in any given month, but it is considerably harder to achieve a minimum 6 percent return *every* month.

We said at the outset that we'd start with a relatively easy target, and gradually work our way to the next plateau. Instead of starting out with a monthly goal of 6%, why not begin with a monthly goal of just 1 percent or 2 percent? A goal like this is unlikely to put much pressure on a trader, which is good—trading can be stressful enough without any additional pressure.

Achieving a goal of just 1 percent per month would put you well ahead of most traders, since the majority of traders lose money. While a goal of 2 percent per month may not sound awe inspiring, if we can achieve it consistently, the annual gain will be just shy of 27 percent—and you'll have outperformed most mutual funds and hedge funds.

If you have successfully achieved your modest goal for three months in a row, raise the goal to the next plateau—from a 1 percent monthly goal to 2 percent, or from 2 percent to 3 percent, and so on. Don't rush through this process; remember, as you gain experience and confidence, you will be a better trader in the future than you are now, and you'll be better suited to more aggressive goals.

Here is the breakdown of monthly goals and their annual equivalents (again, please note that some numbers are rounded, but this has no material effect on the results):

> 1 percent every month = 13 percent annual return
> 2 percent every month = 27 percent annual return
> 3 percent every month = 42 percent annual return
> 4 percent every month = 60 percent annual return
> 5 percent every month = 79 percent annual return
> 6 percent every month = 100 percent annual return
> 7 percent every month = 125 percent annual return
> 8 percent every month = 151 percent annual return
> 9 percent every month = 181 percent annual return
> 10 percent every month = 214 percent annual return

By the time you work your way up to consistent monthly returns of 3 percent and then 4 percent, you'll be putting up respectable numbers, and you'll have gained the benefit of months of experience.

At this point, you'll no longer be like that teenage driver with a learner's permit; instead, you'll be more like a driver who is comfortable and confident behind the wheel, in complete control of your vehicle, with the ability to anticipate trouble before it happens. You will have progressed to a higher plateau.

Of course, there will still be goals for which to strive. If you can achieve consistent monthly gains of 5 percent or 6 percent, you will have truly joined the elite. At this point, you can continue to increase your goals, or perhaps you will have found your "comfort zone." Remember, you don't have to continually increase your goals if you don't feel that you're ready to do so—or if you just don't want to. Your personal comfort with your goal should also be a consideration.

WHAT HAPPENS WHEN I REACH MY GOAL?

Once you've achieved your goal, you don't have to stop trading, but you can take precautions to safeguard your gains. In trading, we use a stop on every trade to limit losses and protect gains. Why not use that same philosophy to protect your monthly returns?

For instance, assume that a trader's goal is a consistent monthly profit of 5 percent. After reaching this goal, she continues trading, and her gain for the month climbs to 10 percent. The trader now calculates a "stop" for the entire account, at the point where the gain was equal to 5 percent. If the monthly gain falls back from 10 percent to 5 percent, she stops trading for the month, and has still achieved her monthly goal. She can continue trading in a demo account for the remainder of the month.

What if you encounter problems and can't meet your objective? If you are consistently failing to meet your goals, they may be too aggressive. Try for an easier target. If things get really tough, cease live trading and switch to a demo account until you regain your footing. Some traders feel that demo trading is beneath them, but sometimes you have to sacrifice your ego if you're serious about making money as a trader. Don't allow foolish pride to stand in the way of your long-term success.

CHAPTER 18

The Forex Playing Field

If you watch and understand American football, you know the subtleties of the sport. You understand the importance of intelligent play calling, the deception of a disguised blitz, and the unique role of special teams players.

If you don't understand, you are watching a lot of big men running around and crashing into each other.

If you watch and understand auto racing, you know about fuel mileage strategy, the aerodynamics of "drafting" at 200 miles per hour, and the effect of an extra quarter pound of air pressure in the right rear tire.

If you don't understand, you are watching a lot of cars running around in a circle.

If you understand the dynamics of the forex playing field, you understand the ability to calculate odds, the consequences of short-term trading, and the importance of interest rate differentials.

If you don't understand, you are playing with fire.

EVENING THE ODDS

Trading can be difficult, and in an effort to make it easier, some traders resort to taking very quick exits. "*It's hard to earn 100 pips,*" goes the rationale, "*I'll just try to make 10 pips on each trade.*" It seems to make sense; surely, it is easier to earn 10 pips than it is to earn 50 or 100 pips. The trader seeks to win by playing it safe, which would seem to be a commendable trait in the trading world.

What if I told you that instead of making things easier, this trader is in fact making his life more difficult? In order to understand why, we need to delve a little deeper into game theory.

THE HOUSE HAS THE EDGE

Imagine a roulette wheel in a casino. You walk up to the table and place a bet on either red or black. What are your chances of success?

If you've never played roulette, you might think the odds are 50–50. After all, half of the numbered pockets are red, and the other half are black, right?

Wrong. In addition to the red and black pockets, there is at least one pocket that is neither red nor black. This "zero" pocket tilts the odds slightly against our player.

In European roulette there is only one zero pocket, giving the house a slight advantage. On this table, the odds are about 53:47 *against* our player. American roulette wheels have two 0s, zero and double zero, and this increases the house advantage to about 5.3 percent. This further stacks the odds against our player, reducing his chances for success.

In the world of forex trading, the zero pockets represent the spread. The odds are always going to be at least slightly in favor of the "house," which in this case is the market maker. The wider the spread, the more "zero pockets" the trader must overcome. Just as each additional zero pocket lowers the roulette player's chances of success, every additional pip in the spread lessens the trader's chances of success.

MAKE THE PLAYING FIELD BIGGER

In the forex market, the house determines the spread, which is the equivalent of the "zero pockets" in roulette. We have no control over the spread—it is determined by the market maker alone, just as the casino determines the number of zero pockets on a roulette wheel.

Ah, but what if we could control the number of red pockets and black pockets? Suppose we were to greatly increase the number of red and black pockets on the roulette wheel, and at the same time keep the number of zero pockets steady.

What effect would this have on the odds? The odds of winning at roulette would improve, because the zero pockets would make up a smaller percentage of the potential outcomes.

As long as there are zero pockets on the wheel, the odds will never be in our favor. But by adding additional red and black pockets to the wheel, we would lessen the casino's advantage and push the odds closer to 50–50. The more red and black pockets we add, the better our chances become. In a sense, we would be making the wheel—which is in this case the "playing field"—bigger.

Of course, we can't add pockets to a roulette wheel. Casinos are too smart to allow us to dilute their edge. While that edge is not overwhelming, it is enough to guarantee that the casino will win more often than they will lose, over a large enough sample of spins.

But in the world of forex trading, we *can* increase the size of the playing field, and thereby improve our chances of trading success. And unlike in a casino, we will not be forcefully removed from the premises for doing so!

How is this done? We make the playing field larger by using wider exits and stops, by using longer time frames, and by trying for larger gains. You've seen the techniques outlined in this book, so let me ask you this: Am I ever shooting for a 10-pip gain?

BUT THE OTHER TRADING INSTRUCTOR SAID...

No, but I know that many traders are seeking exactly that. In fact, some prominent trading instructors are teaching their students to seek only a small 10- or 15-pip gain before exiting the trade. What is their motivation for teaching people to trade this way?

Well, perhaps your "trading coach" has asked you to open an account at a particular broker or market maker. If so, you may have signed an "*introducing broker*" waiver that allows said trading coach to collect a small cash payment every time you place a trade. This is his reward for *introducing* you to the market maker.

If you place just a few trades, your trading coach collects just a little money, but if you place *many* trades, the instructor will be handsomely rewarded. So, it's in the *trading coach's* best interest (and the *market maker's* best interest) to have you placing many trades, even though it may not be in *your* best interest. Think about that the next time a so-called trading instructor tries to convince you to shoot for 10 or 15 pips per trade.

LET'S DO THE MATH

What are the odds of success on a trade with a small target? The following example should give the short-term trader an idea of exactly what it is he or she is up against.

Let's assume for the purpose of this example that we are trading a currency pair that has a 3-pip spread, since a spread of that size is very common in the forex market.

Our trader just wants to gain 10 pips. That should be easy, right? It's understood that the trader will lose the spread (3 pips) upon entering the trade. So, in order to turn a profit of 10 pips, the trader actually needs the exchange rate to move 13 pips in his or her favor:

$$10 + 3 = 13$$

Now that we know what is required to create a winning trade, let's see what would have to happen to create an equivalent loss. This is how we will determine the odds of success or failure.

In order to generate a loss of 10 pips, the trader would only need an adverse move of 7 pips. This is because a loss of 3 pips is incurred immediately upon entering the trade, again due to the 3-pip spread.

$$10 - 3 = 7$$

We've determined that our trader needs a positive move of 13 pips to gain 10 pips, but an adverse move of just 7 pips will result in an equivalent loss of 10 pips. The "raw odds" of 10-pip win versus a 10-pip loss for this trade can be expressed as:

$$13/7 = 1.857 : 1$$

The odds of success in this case are 1.857:1, or nearly 2:1 against. That's a real eye-opener, isn't it? Now you know why it's so difficult to make money trading for small gains—the playing field is too small! This is the equivalent of betting "red" on the roulette wheel, when nearly two-thirds of the pockets are either black or zero pockets.

We can certainly improve the odds of any trade by using good strategies and solid risk management, but it's hard to see how an individual can overcome these initial "raw" odds on a consistent basis. If you've tried to trade this way and failed, now you know why. You're making the market maker rich, and you might be making an introducing broker rich, but chances are you are one of the many forex traders who lose money.

CHANGING THE EQUATION

How can we rearrange the odds so that we can have a better chance to win at forex trading? How can we level the playing field? By making the playing field larger. You see, if we are aiming for larger gains, the spread becomes a less significant portion of the trade. It's the same as adding more black and red pockets to the roulette wheel; unlike roulette, we can choose the size of the playing field in forex trading.

Let's review the earlier trading situation, only this time we'll make the playing field larger. Once again, we'll assume a spread of 3 pips, only this time the trader will be trying to gain 100 pips instead of just 10 pips. In order to turn a profit of 100 pips, the trader actually needs the exchange rate to move 103 pips in his or her favor:

$$100 + 3 = 103$$

In order to generate a loss of 100 pips, the trader would only need an adverse move of only 97 pips. This is because a loss of 3 pips is incurred immediately upon entering the trade.

$$100 - 3 = 97$$

We've determined that the trader needs a positive move of 103 pips to gain 100 pips, but an adverse move of just 97 pips will result in a loss of 100 pips. The "raw odds" of 100-pip win versus a 100-pip loss for this trade can be expressed as:

$$103/97 = 1.06 : 1$$

The odds are now much better, as they are closer to 50–50. As we said earlier, as long as there is a spread, the odds at the beginning of every trade will be less than 50–50. However, if we are using good trading techniques and risk management, or if we are collecting interest on the trade, we can overcome these slightly negative odds.

Now I'm not saying that you have to shoot for gains of 100 pips or more on every trade. The point is to understand that when the playing field is larger in forex trading, the odds of success improve considerably. Also, traders who are aiming for greater gains tend to hold their trades longer, and consequently they enter trades (and pay the spread) less frequently.

Your market maker and your introducing broker may love you less, but your account balance will appreciate it. In the end, you are the only one who either enjoys the gains or suffers the losses in your account.

WHY DOESN'T EVERYONE DO IT?

So why doesn't everybody trade for larger gains? Why do so many traders fall into the trap of trading against staggering odds? There are a couple of possible answers:

1. They don't understand that they are stacking the odds against them-selves.
2. They have harmful preconceived notions about the nature of trading itself.

The problem is that trading isn't always what we believe it to be, or wish it were. I know exactly what I would like trading to be, and here it is: I'd wake up in the morning, trade for an hour, make a ton of money, close my positions, and do whatever I please for the rest of the day. Trading would be like a video game that we could play anytime we please. The more we play the game, the more points we score. We could be rich beyond our wildest dreams, with minimal effort.

That would be ideal in my opinion, but you may have noticed that these strategies do not allow for this. That's because strategies need to work in the *real* trading world, not in some fantasy world of our dreams. The problem is that many traders don't know that their misconceptions about trading are not based on facts. They are trading a market that exists in their dreams, not in reality.

HUGE GAINS WITH MINIMAL EFFORT!

How do we acquire counterproductive attitudes toward trading? My guess is the worst culprits are infomercials that tout huge gains in just minutes a day. You may have seen these long-form commercials, often designed to appear as legitimate television shows, where wide-eyed investors proudly proclaim that they made huge gains with minimal effort.

Huge gains with minimal effort.

It sounds good, and that is no coincidence. You are being told *exactly* what you want to hear. Instead of telling you what you'd like to hear, I'm going to tell you the truth—trading is hard work. Short-term traders are stacking the odds against themselves. There is no such thing as a huge gain with minimal effort.

When I explained that we need to make the playing field larger, and thereby hold our trades longer, this was probably not what you wanted to hear. Why is that? Because we want huge gains with minimal effort.

Why are the airwaves filled with promises of huge gains with minimal effort? Because salesmen know exactly what you want to hear, and they know how to get you to write a big check. Whenever someone tells you exactly what you want to hear, run in the other direction as quickly as possible.

WHAT WE CAN LEARN FROM THE "SMART MONEY"

Think about the way so-called "smart money" approaches trading in this market. Do hedge funds and institutional traders chase after 10- or 15-pip gains? Of course not—they understand the dynamics that are at work here. Not only are they not interested in 10-pip gains, they're not chasing after 100-pip gains either. Many of these "big fish" are only satisfied with gains of *thousands* of pips—trades that push the odds of success as close to 50–50 as possible.

Not only do the institutional traders understand the value of playing on a larger field, they set up their trades so that they can collect interest to boot—thereby increasing their odds to *better than 50–50!* If this were a casino, they'd be tossed out immediately. Now you know why they are called the "smart money"!

NOW GET OUT THERE AND WIN

The good news is that we can trade just like the smart money and avoid trading, well, the other way. Now that you understand the dynamics of the forex playing field, you know more about trading than most of the people who will come, fail, and go without ever understanding the nature of the game they are playing—not a game in the context of something that is not to be taken seriously, but a game that is meant to be *played to win*.

What does *playing to win* mean to you? Does it mean that you'll do things your way, play the game on your own terms, and if everything works out, that's fine? Or does it mean you're willing to do *whatever it takes*—including surrendering your preconceived notions about the game you are playing—in order to make it to the winner's circle? If you're serious about making real money, you'd better be willing to go that extra mile.

CHAPTER 19

Trading Lessons
from Life

If trading were exactly like real life, then it would be much easier. Unfortunately, trading and the real world differ in many ways. Trading is counter-intuitive because what seems or feels right is often wrong, and vice versa.

For example, when you're shopping and you see that an item you want to buy is available at a low price, that's usually a good thing. In the world of trading, when the price or exchange rate seems cheap, it is not always a bargain—it could mean that there is something wrong.

Although the lessons of life sometimes betray us in the world of trading, there are some aspects of life that can teach us a great deal about trading.

PANIC AT THE BEACH

One of my best friends in the world is a guy named Marlio, popularly known as "Mongo" back in high school, who moved west to Los Angeles to pursue a career as a screenwriter.

One time, after giving a seminar in L.A., I caught up with my old friend, and we hit the beach for some body surfing in Malibu. We rode some nice waves, and as the day progressed, they became bigger and rougher.

Eventually, I caught a big wave and sailed toward the beach. Suddenly, the surf became violent and slammed me against the ocean floor. I could feel the crush of the wild surf as I was tossed about like laundry on a spin cycle.

223

After being thoroughly "Maytaged," I struggled to reach the surface. As I finally caught my breath, the reality sank in. I had lost my swim trunks. I was naked in public, on a crowded beach in sunny California!

Staggered by the giant wave, I lurched around in a futile attempt to retrieve my trunks, which were slowly drifting out to sea. Mongo was of no help, as he was doubled over by convulsions of laughter. Hey, if you can't laugh at your friend, who is involuntarily committing indecent exposure at the moment, whom can you laugh at?

By now the people on the beach had noticed the naked man in their midst, chasing his pants among the waves. When I finally tracked down and donned the errant trunks, a loud cheer went up from the beach.

Later, at a restaurant overlooking the Pacific, we roared with laughter as we recounted the events of the day. The drinks flowed as the sun sank into the ocean.

What does this have to do with trading? Well, let me break it to you gently: Bad things are going to happen to you—in life and in trading. Things will go wrong. Trading errors will occur. Your computer system will crash. Markets will tease, taunt, and humble you. At times, you will feel as though you are about to lose your mind.

When presented with these challenges, we have a choice—we can hang our heads in defeat, or we can choose to believe that defeat is only a temporary condition, and that there is no such thing as permanent defeat. We can choose to play the role of the victim when things go wrong, or we can choose to laugh at ourselves. We can learn not to take ourselves too seriously.

When things go awry, try to keep this thought in mind:

> "It's not what happens to you, it's how you react to what happens to you that determines success or failure."

THE ENDLESS TOURNAMENT

Joey is another one of my great friends. Joey and I played Little League baseball together when we were both eight years old, and we are still close friends to this day.

Joe and I fancy ourselves to be (very) amateur athletes. Despite a total lack of understanding of the rules of the game, we decided to take up racquetball—and we were awful. But we played racquetball at a similar level of awfulness, so the games were fun.

We decided to play a mini-tournament; we just needed to decide on the duration of the contest. Best of three? Best of seven, perhaps? I came up with an idea.

"How about first one to win 100 games wins."

Joey laughed. "Sure, why not?"

So we started to play. The more we played, the better we became at playing. Joe would come up with a new serve that I couldn't return, and he'd beat me for a while. Then I'd find a way to counter him, and I'd pull back into the lead.

Every time one of us would come up with a better shot, or a better play, the other would learn it and we were back to even again. We constantly raised the bar, challenging each other relentlessly.

Then a funny thing happened; I noticed that we were no longer awful at playing racquetball. Not great, but not awful.

As of this writing, we've played a total of 120 games over the past seven months. Joe has won 60 games so far, and I've won 60. We still play at a similar level, but now we both make ridiculous, gravity-defying plays and hit seemingly impossible shots on a regular basis.

How does this relate to trading? You can learn faster if you can find a partner, a friend, or group of friends who share a similar interest and have a similar level of understanding. You can share information and techniques, test each other's knowledge, and bounce ideas off of each other. You can push each other, and together you can accelerate the journey through the learning curve.

Support groups such as chat rooms can be extremely helpful. Individuals can also form their own trading groups, or keep in touch through instant messaging. Once you've found the right person or persons, you'll be amazed at how quickly the pieces of the puzzle can fall into place.

SUMMARY

There are many things in life that traders can use to draw inspiration. Perhaps you've heard the story of the farmer who learned to trade futures in order to hedge his crops. After becoming a proficient trader, John W. Henry left the farming profession. He is now one of the world's most successful hedge fund managers, owns a futures company, and is a part owner of the Boston Red Sox. Mr. Henry considers himself to be a trend-following trader.

You may have heard of the gentleman whose first trade was made with $3,000 he borrowed from his credit card. Today, multibillionaire

Bruce Kovner is a fixture on the annual list of top-earning hedge fund managers. At one point, before conquering the world of trading, Mr. Kovner actually drove a taxicab in New York and studied music at Juilliard.

The point is: with persistence, determination, and the right attitude, anyone can succeed in the world of trading.

CHAPTER 20

What You Don't Know Can Hurt You

H ere's a little section of the book that will ruffle a few feathers. If you ever hear that I've gone missing under mysterious circumstances, it'll probably be due to of the contents of this chapter.

These next few pages aren't intended to scare you, but to educate you to some of the realities of the trading business. I want you to know about the pitfalls that are lurking out there, waiting for the unsuspecting and the uninitiated. If I can keep you on the right path and prevent you from being drawn into these traps, your chances of success will increase dramatically. To be forewarned is to be forearmed.

You will often hear of spectacular returns. You will hear salespeople bragging about 90 percent winning trades, 95 percent winning trades, and so on. You will hear claims that it is possible to win many consecutive trades on a consistent basis.

And what could be wrong with winning? It feels good to win, right? Well, the salesperson who is trying to sell you a product or service that promises such a high percentage of winning trades (or in some cases promises a ridiculous number of consecutive winners) is counting on your desire to win to short-circuit your thought process.

It is easy to obtain 90 percent winning trades and still lose money. Conversely, there are many successful traders who place more losing trades than winning trades. The percentage of winning trades has nothing to do with the ultimate success of the trader. Most references to a percentage of winning trades are merely a sales tactic, which is intended to appeal to the trader's desire to "win."

SARCASM ALERT!

Do you want to know how to create a high percentage of winning trades? Why not simply trade without stops (breaking every rule of risk management, which will surely lead to losses) and take profits quickly? That way, we can hold on to every trade until it either turns profitable or creates a margin call.

If this sounds ridiculous, that's because it is, but the point must be made. It saddens me to tell you that this is exactly how many people try to trade. They'll get lucky for a while, putting up some nice returns at first, and then they will blow a hole in the account with one big loss. Their percentage of winners versus losers will still be impressive, but their account equity will be severely damaged.

People actually teach so-called trading techniques that promise many consecutive winning trades. I have heard promises of 20 consecutive winners, 50 consecutive winners, and more.

This would be similar to flipping a coin 50 times with the expectation that the coin will land with the "head" facing upward every single time. Not only is this trader almost guaranteed to lose money in the long run, but to add insult to injury, he or she actually paid someone to learn techniques that are sure to result in losses.

KNOW WHEN TO RETREAT

Fixation on the percentage of winning trades versus losing trades is like a sickness, and I'm determined to cure this rampant disease within our lifetimes.

I want you to think of yourself as a general, fighting a war. Your most important assets are your soldiers. You want to use them judiciously. When it is time to attack, you send them off to battle but if the battle is lost, you must retreat. Otherwise, you will needlessly sacrifice the lives of your troops and weaken your overall forces. Your goal is not to win every battle, but to win the war instead.

Trading is much the same way. In order to win the war, you have to be willing to lose a few battles along the way. Or, more precisely, you have to be willing to deal with small losses to prevent the creation of a large loss.

Most major trading disasters have their genesis in the unwillingness to take a loss, from Nick Leeson's destruction of Barings Bank to the Long-Term Capital Management hedge fund fiasco. There are countless other examples of major trading disasters that begin with the failure to take a strategic loss.

THE "95 PERCENT WINNERS STRATEGY"

To bolster my point, I opened a demo account and proceeded to place trades using a "strategy" of holding on to losses until the trade turned positive, and then taking very small gains (see Figure 20.1).

I placed a total of 20 trades, with 19 "winners" and 1 loss, resulting in a success rate of 95 percent. One might think that a success rate of 95 percent would certainly lead to a nice profit, but as you can see, this is not necessarily the case.

Because this trader was too quick to take profits and too willing to hold losses, this so-called strategy resulted in a loss, despite the lofty winning percentage. Unfortunately, this scenario is all too common.

Hopefully, this little exercise will cure all of us once and for all of our tendency to be impressed by sales tactics that present an abnormally skewed ratio of winners versus losers. If we allow salespeople to cloud our vision with unrealistic or impossible dreams, it will only delay our ultimate goal of trading successfully in the real world.

Closed Positions (20)									
Ticket	Account	Currency	Amt K	B/S	Open	Close	P/L	Gross P/L	
5136521	00296793	EUR/USD	100	B	1.2623	1.2624	1	10.00	
5136528	00296793	USD/JPY	100	B	113.34	113.35	1	8.82	
5136658	00296793	GBP/USD	100	S	1.8392	1.8391	1	10.00	
5136672	00296793	USD/CHF	100	S	1.2373	1.2372	1	8.08	
5136750	00296793	AUD/USD	100	B	0.7623	0.7624	1	10.00	
5136829	00296793	EUR/GBP	100	B	0.6857	0.6859	2	36.78	
5136844	00296793	NZD/USD	100	S	0.6396	0.6395	1	10.00	
5137249	00296793	NZD/USD	100	S	0.6389	0.6388	1	10.00	
5137255	00296793	USD/JPY	100	S	113.39	113.38	1	8.82	
5137256	00296793	EUR/JPY	100	B	143.11	143.12	1	8.83	
5137262	00296793	USD/CAD	100	B	1.1071	1.1072	1	9.03	
5137330	00296793	NZD/USD	100	S	0.6384	0.6383	1	10.00	
5137723	00296793	USD/JPY	100	S	113.38	113.37	1	8.82	
5137762	00296793	USD/CAD	100	S	1.1073	1.1072	1	9.03	
5137861	00296793	USD/JPY	100	S	113.33	113.32	1	8.82	
5137990	00296793	USD/JPY	100	S	113.30	113.29	1	8.83	
5139239	00296793	USD/JPY	100	S	113.36	113.34	2	17.65	
5139257	00296793	AUD/USD	100	B	0.7655	0.7656	1	10.00	
5139300	00296793	EUR/USD	100	B	1.2612	1.2614	2	20.00	
5139302	00296793	GBP/USD	100	S	1.8367	1.8404	-37	-370.00	
Total			2,000				-15	-146.49	

FIGURE 20.1 Many traders overestimate the importance of win versus loss percentage. In this case, 19 winning trades and 1 losing trade = 95 percent winning trades. Despite the lofty winning percentage, the overall result is a loss.

Source: Forex Capital Markets (FXCM); www.fxcm.com.

BEWARE THE BACK TESTER

There is nothing wrong with back testing a strategy per se; in fact, back testing can be a valuable tool in strategy development when it is used properly. However, some unscrupulous operators have appropriated this strategy development tool and turned it into a weapon for use against an unsuspecting trading public.

Back testing is the process of optimizing a trading strategy using historical data. Traders back test strategies to determine how well they have worked in the past, with the assumption that what has worked in the past will continue to work in the future.

Since markets are not static, and are constantly evolving and changing, back testing is not a panacea. The past does not equal the future. As markets change, good traders adapt, and the best traders are the ones who adapt quickly.

Because we know what has occurred in the past, it is easy to create strategies that would have been highly successful in the past. Since we can't turn back the clock and trade in the past, these strategies are limited in their usefulness. This hasn't stopped some individuals from marketing these overoptimized, back-tested strategies as current and viable money-making opportunities.

One individual allegedly solicited funds from unsuspecting investors by misrepresenting back tested returns as actual returns. This person is currently the subject of a Commodity Futures Trading Commission complaint, for allegedly having "engaged in the fraudulent solicitation of customers by misrepresenting his past performance."

HYPOTHETICALLY SPEAKING

Other unscrupulous individuals attempt to sell back-tested strategies to the unsuspecting, using impressive-sounding hypothetical returns as a sales tool.

Whenever someone tries to impress you with the alleged returns of a strategy, be sure to ask that person if the results are actual or hypothetical. Too many people assume that hypothetical returns are actual returns, but this simply is not the case.

Hypothetical returns are not created from actual trading, and are usually the result of back testing. Now that we know how easily one can create seemingly impressive results from mere back testing, it becomes apparent that we should never be overly impressed with hypothetical results.

One day far in the future, perhaps mankind will finally perfect the time machine. If that should occur, overoptimized back-tested strategies and hypothetical returns will become valuable indeed. Until then, since we cannot trade the past, the usefulness of these tools is severely limited.

CHAPTER 21

A Tale of
Two Traders

I 've been fortunate enough to trade not only for myself, but also for several hedge funds. Working with hedge funds is terrific—they write big checks and then they leave you alone. Trading for individuals is hard work—they write small checks and they never leave you alone. If you want to trade for others, institutional money is the way to go.

There is a lot of institutional money out there, looking for a home. Hedge funds have expanded tremendously in the past few years, with assets under management skyrocketing from about $500 billion in the year 2000 to over $1.5 trillion in 2006. These figures will likely continue to grow in the future. The upshot of this is that some hedge funds literally have more money to invest than they can reasonably handle, and they might "farm out" some of these assets to individuals like you and me.

If you can establish a reasonable track record, you might be able to convince a hedge fund to allow you to trade some of their funds. What constitutes a good track record? The answer may be different from what you believe.

INDIVIDUALS VERSUS INSTITUTIONS

If you want to trade for individuals, you'll often be asked, "How much money will you make for me?" This is indicative of how most individual traders think; they are more concerned about reward than they are about risk. Individuals ask questions like, "How long will it take to double my money?" and "When will my account reach $1 million?"

Also, if you are getting started in managing money for individuals, be prepared to answer a lot of questions and do a lot of hand-holding. You may find yourself so busy explaining your work to your clients that it interferes with your trading.

Take these words to heart: There is an old saying in this business, "*Amateurs are concerned with how much money they can make, and professionals are concerned with how much money they can lose*." Write that on a sticky pad and put it on your computer monitor.

No hedge fund representative has ever asked me, "Ed, how much money are you going to earn for us this year?" No, the question you'll hear from a hedge fund is more likely to be, "What is your biggest drawdown?"

Professional investors do care about how much you can earn, but they care more about how much risk you are willing to take in order to earn that profit. They know from experience that traders who are willing to risk it all will eventually lose it all.

What is a drawdown? It can be best described as a reduction in account equity from a trade or series of trades, usually expressed as a percentage from peak to trough. So, if a trader begins with $50,000, and his account value falls to $40,000 after a series of trades, we could say that the trader has suffered a drawdown of 20 percent.

THE DIFFERENCE BETWEEN AMATEURS AND PROFESSIONALS

When judging your performance record, an institutional investment company will first determine whether your returns are due to your brilliant decision making or if they are a result of excessive risk.

Imagine two traders, both with starting equity of $50,000. Trader A was able to double the initial investment to $100,000, a gain of 100 percent, although along the way he suffered a drawdown of 50 percent.

Trader B's account rose to $60,000, a gain of just 20 percent, and his worst drawdown was just 2 percent of the account's value. Which trader is the better of the two?

Trader A had the larger return by far, but he is an accident waiting to happen. Anyone who is willing to lose 50 percent, or half of his account, is a good candidate to lose it all. This trader probably holds on to losing trades, or even adds to them, which is the trademark of failure in this business.

Trader B is by far the superior trader, because he was able to achieve substantial gains with just a minimal drawdown. Typically, at this point the hedge fund will want to know how much money Trader B could comfortably trade, and then give him a percentage of that amount. The hedge fund will monitor his returns and allocate more capital if Trader B can continue to put up solid, consistent numbers.

Trader A's gains were two times the size of his worst drawdown, while Trader B's gains were 10 times larger than his worst drawdown. Based on this result, Trader B is an excellent candidate to trade institutional money. Trader A can look forward to competing in the "King of the Tiny Accounts" contest, since his affinity for risk means that he probably will not have a full-sized account for much longer. Hedge funds will not touch Trader A, because as professional money managers, they have been through this before and are all too familiar with how the story ends—with a devastating loss.

CHAPTER 22

Some Final Thoughts

There are so many different aspects to trading, it's impossible to cover each and every one in the space allotted here. In this book we've attempted to cover the important technical aspects of trading from the forex point of view, in terms of practical strategies and trading methodologies. At this time, I'd like to touch upon some important points that you may find useful in your trading.

A GOOD TRADE IS NOT THE SAME THING AS A WINNING TRADE

Always remember that, in trading, the ends do not justify the means. Or to be more precise, the outcome of your trade does not necessarily justify the method used to achieve that outcome. Some traders take the attitude that as long as the trade is a winner, there is justification no matter what rules were broken along the way.

But the fact is that a winning trade is not always a good trade, and a good trade is not always a winning trade. It's possible to do everything wrong and still achieve a winning result on a particular trade, just as it's possible to do everything correctly and still lose on any given trade.

Would you rather be a good trader or a lucky trader? Strive to be a good trader, because anyone can be a lucky trader—for a while. Don't judge your trading on any particular result, but on whether you are following proper procedure. Did you follow a predetermined plan? Did you place the stop correctly and sensibly? Do you have an exit strategy?

If you are doing all of these things correctly, and still are not trading successfully, at least you will then be able to determine that the problem lies not with your execution but with the plan. Plans can be modified.

PROPER EXECUTION IS CRITICAL

If the problem lies with us—if we always get out too soon, or if we trade without stops, or if we just enter and exit on a whim – then we'll eventually fail, even though the original plan itself may not be at fault. A good plan is useless if it's being executed improperly.

This is where so many traders go wrong. They want to succeed so they create a plan; then they randomly change the plan because they don't have the discipline to follow it. Then when they fail, they blame the plan. The fault is not with the plan but in their failure to execute properly.

Such a trader moves from one technique to the next (because the techniques "don't work") when in reality they have no way of knowing if their plan works. When you successfully follow your plan properly, do everything that you can to reinforce that behavior, regardless of the outcome of any particular trade.

The outcome of any single trade is not within the realm of your control, but you can control your ability to follow a plan. So we concern ourselves with the things that we can control (planning and execution) and worry less about things that are beyond our control (the result of any given individual trade).

Conversely, never congratulate yourself for a "winning" trade outcome that comes as a result of ignoring your plan or trading without a plan. Instead, consider yourself lucky and realize that in the long run, you will not succeed in this manner. Remember, if you consistently break the rules, eventually the rules will break you.

TAKE RESPONSIBILITY FOR YOUR ACTIONS

Some traders love to place blame. They would have you believe that their poor trading records are due to manipulation on the part of market makers or institutions or some other outside influence. They will tell you that their lack of success is certainly no fault of their own.

Dodging blame may be an effective technique for dealing with many aspects of life, for example, at work or with your significant other, but it is not conducive to good trading.

The trouble is this: If we deflect blame, then there is no need for us to change. The fault lies with someone else, so therefore there is no need for us to grow and learn. But does your account balance care who is at fault if you lose money?

Accept responsibility for every single trade that you place. You accept credit for the winning trades, don't you? Then accept blame for the losing trades as well. When we take responsibility for our actions, we control the situation. Individuals who fail to take responsibility for their own trades will never succeed in any trading environment.

KEEP IT SIMPLE

As mentioned earlier, many traders who fail to follow a plan often discard that plan because they feel it "doesn't work," and then move on to another plan. One thing that I've noticed, especially among highly intelligent traders, is that they feel that a plan must be complicated in order to succeed.

They become drawn into a world of increasingly obscure and complicated techniques, use super-secret indicators, and keep burrowing deeper into the fringes as if searching for some secret that has eluded them. The more complicated the plan is, the better it must be, right?

Of course, this is not the case. Can complicated techniques work? Absolutely! But simple techniques can work just as well, if they are executed properly.

Think of a trading strategy as if it were a machine; if it has fewer moving parts, then there are fewer parts that can break, and fewer things that can go wrong with it.

It is always a fun intellectual exercise to learn about various and complex trading methods, but this does not mean that simple methods cannot work. If you have faced difficulty while using simple methods, there is a good chance that either the plan was not a good one or the plan was not properly executed.

PHYSICAL VERSUS MENTAL

I don't think that any overview of trading would be complete without touching on the subjects of physical fitness and mental attitude. In this profession, it's easy to wear down physically and mentally, especially when dealing with a 24-hour market. It's really important to get some exercise whenever possible, because the physical stimulation can actually increase your mental sharpness and improve your decision-making capabilities.

Try to get to the gym or at least get some kind of exercise every day; you'll feel better, and chances are you'll trade better, too. It's not healthy to sit at a computer all day every day, so be sure to plan an intraday break from trading.

There are plenty of books and materials available that are designed to improve mental attitudes, and you should approach these with an open mind. I was surprised to learn that many successful traders enjoy these types of materials. It's been my experience that the beliefs of the reader will greatly impact the results, or lack thereof, of the study of the materials.

What I mean by that is if you think that reading these types of books will have a positive impact on your trading, you are correct, and if you believe they will not, you are also correct. This is why it is necessary to have an open mind when studying these subjects. I've always favored the works of Napoleon Hill, and there are many other authors of this type.

Remember, if you allow yourself to get too tired and to wear down, your body will rebel against this behavior. Psychologists believe that individuals who work too hard often subconsciously sabotage their own work, in order to get away from the work and back to a sense of normalcy.

This occurs to traders all the time, in the form of a trading error. If you find yourself sitting at your computer for 16 hours a day, placing endless trades, be sure to remind yourself of why you began trading in the first place. I'm certain that the idea was to improve your quality of life, not to diminish it. It's like my father says, "Don't forget to enjoy your life!"

IN CLOSING

In closing, I'd like to thank you for taking the time to study and understand these materials. Forex trading offers many advantages, and taking the time to learn how to trade the forex market might be the best trading decision you ever make.

You can learn more about my methods and techniques by visiting www.edponsi.com and www.fxeducator.com and you can contact me at info@fxeducator.com.

I wish you the best of luck on your journey.

Glossary

appreciation When a currency increases in value in response to market demand, it is said to "appreciate."

arbitrage The simultaneous taking of equal and opposite positions in related markets, in order to take advantage of price or interest rate differentials between markets.

ask The quoted price at which an investor can buy a currency pair. This is also known as the "offer" or "asking price."

asset Any item having commercial or exchange value.

asset allocation Practice that divides funds among different investments to achieve diversification for risk management purposes.

balance of trade The value of a country's exports minus its imports.

bar chart A type of chart that consists of four major price points: the high and the low prices, which form the vertical bar; the opening price, which is marked with a small horizontal line to the left of the bar; and the closing price, which is marked with a small horizontal line of the right of the bar.

base currency The first member of a currency pair is the base currency. The base currency is the currency against which exchange rates are quoted. Examples: USD/CHF, the U.S. dollar is the base currency; AUD/USD, the Australian dollar is the base currency.

bid The quoted price at which an investor can sell a currency pair. This is also known as the "bid price" or "bid rate".

bretton woods   The site of conference in 1944 that led to the establishment of the postwar foreign exchange system. The conference resulted in a fixed exchange rate system that allowed only small fluctuations of currencies to gold or the U.S. dollar.

cable   Trading term that refers to the Great Britain pound/U.S. dollar exchange rate. The exchange rate was originally transmitted via a transatlantic cable beginning in the mid-1800s.

candlestick chart   A form of Japanese charting that has become popular in the West, which displays the open, high, low, and closing prices. A narrow line (the "wick") represents the day's price range, and a wider body marks the area between the open and the closing prices.

central bank   The government or governmental authority that manages a country's monetary policy. For example, the U.S. central bank is the Federal Reserve, and Japan's central bank is the Bank of Japan.

closed position   Exposures in the currency markets that no longer exist. To close a position, a trader must buy or sell an equal amount of the open position. The position is now referred to as "flat."

counter currency   The second member of a currency pair is the counter currency. Examples: USD/CHF, the Swiss franc is the counter currency; AUD/USD, the U.S. dollar is the counter currency.

cross currency pairs   A pair of currencies that does not include the U.S. dollar. For example: AUD/CAD or GBP/JPY.

day trading   A style of trading where positions are opened and closed during the same day.

depreciation   A fall in the value of a currency due to market forces. When a currency falls in value in response to market supply, it is said to "depreciate."

deficit   A negative balance of trade or payments.

devaluation   The deliberate downward adjustment of a currency's value, normally by official announcement.

downtick   A new price quote at an exchange rate lower than the preceding quote.

economic indicator A statistic that measures strength or weakness in a particular area of an economy. Common indicators include nonfarm payroll (NFP), gross domestic product (GDP), and consumer price index (CPI).

euro The currency of the European Monetary Union (EMU).

European Central Bank (ECB) The Central Bank for the European Monetary Union (EMU).

European Monetary Union Those countries that have agreed to use the euro as their principal currency.

execution The process of completing or filling an order.

Federal Reserve The central bank of the United States.

fill The process of completing a customer's order to buy or sell a currency pair.

flat Term that describes a trading account with no market exposure.

FOMC Federal Open Market Committee, the policy committee in the Federal Reserve System that sets short-term monetary policy objectives for the Fed.

fundamental analysis Analysis of economic and political information with the objective of determining future movements in the forex market.

G7 The seven leading industrial countries, consisting of the United States, Germany, Japan, France, the United Kingdom, Canada, and Italy.

gross domestic product (GDP) The total value of goods and services produced by a country.

hedge A position or combination of positions that reduces the risk of a primary position; a transaction that reduces the risk on an existing investment position.

inflation An economic condition whereby prices for consumer goods rise, resulting in a decline in the purchasing power of money.

Interbank   A network of major banks around the world that trade currencies among each other and on behalf of their clients.

interbank rates   The foreign exchange rates that major banks quote each other for currency transactions.

intervention   Action by a central bank to affect the value of its currency through buying or selling in the open market.

kiwi   Slang term for the New Zealand dollar.

leading indicators   A composite index of various economic indicators designed to predict economic activity six to nine months into the future.

LIBOR   The London Interbank Offered Rate. Banks use LIBOR when borrowing from another bank.

liquidity   The ability of a market to accept large transactions with minimal to no impact on price stability.

long position   In foreign exchange, when a currency pair is bought, it is understood that the base currency in the pair is "long," and the counter currency is "short."

lot   Standard unit of measurement for position size in the foreign exchange markets.

margin   The required equity that an investor must deposit to collateralize a position.

margin call   A request from a broker or dealer for additional funds or collateral to guarantee performance on a position that has moved against the customer.

market maker   A dealer who regularly quotes both bid and ask prices and is prepared to make a two-sided market for any financial instrument.

market risk   Exposure to changes in exchange rates.

momentum   The tendency of a currency pair to continue movement in a single direction.

net position   An amount or position of a currency that has not yet been offset by opposing transactions.

offer   The quoted price at which an investor can buy a currency pair. This is also known as the "ask" or "ask rate."

offsetting transaction   A trade that serves to cancel or offset some or all of the market risk of an open position.

open order   Buy or sell order that remains in effect until executed or canceled by the customer.

open position   Any position (long or short) that is subject to market fluctuations and has not been closed out by a corresponding opposite transaction.

pip   The smallest unit of price for any currency.

price transparency   Describes quotes to which every market participant has equal access.

profit/loss (P/L)   The actual "realized" gain or loss resulting from closed positions, plus the theoretical "unrealized" gain or loss on open positions.

quote   An indicative market price, normally used for information purposes only.

resistance   Price level at which technical analysts note persistent selling of a currency pair.

rally   A recovery in the exchange rate after a period of decline.

range   The difference between the highest and lowest price recorded during a given trading session.

risk management   Trading techniques designed to reduce and/or control exposure to financial risk.

short position   An investment position that benefits from a decline in market price. When the base currency in the pair is sold, the position is said to be short.

spot price   The current market price. Settlement of spot transactions usually occurs within two business days.

spread   The difference between the bid and ask prices.

sterling   Trading term that refers to the Great Britain pound.

stop loss order   Order type whereby an open position is automatically liquidated at a specific price. Often used to minimize exposure to losses.

support level   Price level at which technical analysts note persistent buying of a currency pair.

technical analysis   An effort to forecast future market prices by analyzing charts and data.

uptick   A new price quote at an exchange rate higher than the preceding quote.

volatility   Statistical measure of the change in price of a currency pair over a given time period.

whipsaw   Slang for a highly volatile market condition, where a sharp price movement is quickly followed by a sharp reversal.

Index